# WORKS BY ERNEST HEMINGWAY (BOOK GUIDE)

Books LLC®, Reference Series, Memphis, USA, 2011. ISBN: 9781155964126. www.booksllc.net. Copyright: http://creativecommons.org/licenses/by-sa/3.0/deed.en

## Table of Contents

| | |
|---|---|
| 88 Poems | 1 |
| A Clean, Well-Lighted Place | 2 |
| A Day's Wait | 3 |
| A Farewell to Arms | 3 |
| A Moveable Feast | 5 |
| A Simple Enquiry | 6 |
| A Very Short Story | 6 |
| Across the River and into the Trees | 7 |
| Big Two-Hearted River | 9 |
| Cat in the Rain | 10 |
| Dateline: Toronto | 10 |
| Death in the Afternoon | 11 |
| Ernest Hemingway | 12 |
| Ernest Hemingway: The Collected Stories | 23 |
| Ernest Hemingway Selected Letters 1917–1961 | 24 |
| Ernest Hemingway bibliography | 24 |
| Fathers and Sons (short story) | 25 |
| For Whom the Bell Tolls | 25 |
| Green Hills of Africa | 28 |
| Hills Like White Elephants | 29 |
| In Another Country | 31 |
| In Our Time (book) | 31 |
| Indian Camp | 32 |
| Islands in the Stream (novel) | 34 |
| Men Without Women (short story collection) | 35 |
| Nick Adams (character) | 35 |
| Now I Lay Me | 36 |
| Soldier's Home | 36 |
| The Battler | 36 |
| The Capital of the World (short story) | 36 |
| The Complete Short Stories of Ernest Hemingway | 36 |
| The Dangerous Summer | 37 |
| The Doctor and the Doctor's Wife | 38 |
| The End of Something | 38 |
| The Fifth Column and the First Forty-Nine Stories | 39 |
| The Gambler, the Nun, and the Radio | 40 |
| The Garden of Eden | 40 |
| The Killers (short story) | 41 |
| The Nick Adams Stories (book) | 42 |
| The Old Man and the Sea | 42 |
| The Short Happy Life of Francis Macomber | 44 |
| The Snows of Kilimanjaro | 45 |
| The Snows of Kilimanjaro (book) | 46 |
| The Snows of Kilimanjaro (film) | 46 |
| The Sun Also Rises | 47 |
| The Torrents of Spring | 54 |
| The Undefeated (short story) | 55 |
| Three Stories and Ten Poems | 55 |
| To Have and Have Not | 55 |
| True at First Light | 57 |
| Under Kilimanjaro | 61 |
| Up in Michigan | 61 |
| Winner Take Nothing | 62 |

## Introduction

Purchase of this book entitles you to a free trial membership in the publisher's book club at www.booksllc.net. (Time limited offer.) Simply enter the barcode number from the back cover onto the membership form. The book club entitles you to select from hundreds of thousands of books at no additional charge. You can also download a digital copy of this and related books to read on the go. Simply enter the title or subject onto the search form to find them.

Each chapter in this book ends with a URL to a hyperlinked online version. Type the URL exactly as it appears. If you change the URL's capitalization it won't work. Use the online version to access related pages, websites, footnotes, tables, color photos, updates. Click the version history tab to see the chapter's contributors. Click the edit link to suggest changes.

A large and diverse editor base collaboratively wrote the book, not a single author. After a long process of discussion and debate, the chapters gradually took on a neutral point of view reached through consensus. Additional editors expanded and contributed to chapters striving to achieve balance and comprehensive coverage. This reduced the regional or cultural bias found in many other books and provided access and breadth on subject matter otherwise little documented.

## 88 Poems

*88 Poems* is a book of the collected poetry of author Ernest Hemingway, published in 1979. It includes a number of poems published in magazines, the poems which appeared in Hemingway's first book, *Three Stories and Ten Poems*, and 47 previously unpublished poems that were found in private collections and in the Hemingway papers held by the Kennedy Library.

Source (edited): "http://en.wikipedia.org/wiki/88_Poems"

# A Clean, Well-Lighted Place

"A Clean, Well-Lighted Place" is a short story by American author Ernest Hemingway, first published in 1926. It was later included in his 1933 collection, *Winner Take Nothing*.

## Plot synopsis

*"The old man liked to sit late because he was deaf and now at the night it was quiet and he felt the difference"*. He was drunk as usual. The waiters are chatting about the old man who tried to commit suicide last week. The young waiter has no idea why he wanted to kill himself: *"He was in despair"* (...) *"He has plenty of money"*.

Afterwards in the café, both waiters are talking about the reasons that some old people commit suicide. From this conversation, the reader can gather that the old man who was there last week hanged himself with a rope, and that it was his niece that cut him down. The young waiter again states that the old man who is there tonight should go home because he, the young waiter, wants to go home to his wife. Furthermore, the young waiter cannot understand that both the old man and the older waiter like to stay in the café longer: *"He's lonely. I'm not lonely. I have a wife waiting in bed for me."*- he said. Once again we can see that the young waiter has no regard toward the old, as he describes the old as a *"nasty thing."* The older waiter tries to explain a few things to the younger waiter.

Both waiters are pulling the shutter, only this time they are talking about a matter of being lonely, feeling no fear about going home before usual hours. Young man: *"I'm confidence. I am all confidence."* Then he says that the older waiter has the same things as he, but the older waiter says *"No. I have never had confidence and I am not young (...) I am of those who like to stay late at the café,"* (...) *"With all those who do not want to go to bed. With all those who need a light for the night."* The young waiter seems not to comprehend the idea of a well-lighted and clean place where the old can escape from loneliness. *"..there are shadows of the leaves"*- the older waiter says. *Well-lighted* is a contrast with the darkness of death and bad thoughts. The darkness must be avoided because in the darkness everything is a "nada" (Spanish: 'nothing'). The older waiter stays in case someone needs a lighted cafe in the night, in contrast with a bodega or a bar, which may not be lighted or clean and thus will only increase the loneliness.

The young waiter leaves the scene, and after 'good night,' the older waiter begins a monologue in which "nada [nothing]" replaces words in the Lord's Prayer, and the first line in the Hail Mary prayer.
*Our nada who art in nada, nada be thy name thy kingdom nada thy will be nada in nada as it is in nada. Give us this nada our daily nada and nada us our nada as we nada our nadas and nada us not into nada but deliver us from nada; pues nada [then nothing]. Hail nothing full of nothing, nothing is with thee.*
After that he smiles and goes to stand in front of a bar, which he thinks needs cleaning.
*"What's yours?"* asked the barman. [apparently asking for an order, meaning "What is your drink"]
*"Nada."*
*"Otro loco mas,"* [Another crazy person] said the barman and turned away. The waiter then finally orders a little coffee.

The story ends with these words:
*Now, without thinking further, he would go home to his room. He would lie in the bed and finally, with daylight, he would go to sleep. After all, he said to himself, it's probably only insomnia. Many must have it.*

## Interpretation

Some have argued that Hemingway contrasts light and shadow differentiate the old man and the young people around him, and uses the deafness of the old man as a symbol for his separation from the rest of the world.

In *A Clean Well Lighted Place* Hemingway uses the waiters to judge the old man and portray his views toward the type of drinker he is. As a clean drunk, the man does not spill a drop as he drinks and walks "unsteadily but with dignity" when he finally leaves the café. The waiters talk between themselves as the young waiter asks the old waiter the man's story. He wonders how anyone could sit alone while drinking instead of buying a bottle for himself while drinking in the comfort of his own home. It is then the old waiter who defends the man. The old waiter acknowledges that it is better for the man to have many drinks in public than any drinks in private. In the film version of the story, the old waiter goes to bed alone in his own place with a bottle of alcohol near his nightstand suggesting that he had been speaking from experience while defending the old man.

Another way to analyze the relationships between the men is to compare them as one person. The young waiter complains about having to stick around the café waiting for the man to finish drinking. He claims that he has a wife to go home to and he would rather be in bed than in the café. The old waiter defends the drinking man because he can relate and even see himself in the man. He sympathizes knowing that he, too, prefers a clean well lighted place to drink and will later appreciate such a place in his old drinking age. The old man is in his final years of life and the old waiter recognizes that he soon will have the same fate as the old man. A progression of age is seen among the characters demonstrating the transition from being young and social to aging and feeling lonely. In "A Clean Well Lighted Place," Hemingway portrays a difference in age, experience, and opinion of drinking through the unique characters that could represent a progression of alcoholism.

## Historical reaction by other authors

James Joyce once remarked: "He [Hemingway] has reduced the veil between literature and life, which is what every

writer strives to do. Have you read 'A Clean Well-Lighted Place'?...It is masterly. Indeed, it is one of the best short stories ever written..."
Source (edited): "http://en.wikipedia.org/wiki/A_Clean,_Well-Lighted _Place"

# A Day's Wait

"**A Day's Wait**" is a short story by Ernest Hemingway which appears in *The Snows of Kilimanjaro*, first printed in 1933.

### Synopsis

The story focuses on a nine-year old boy named Schatz and his father. When the boy gets the flu, his temperature rises to 102 degrees. He is very quiet and depressed, finally asking when he will die; he had thought that a 102 degree temperature was lethal because he heard in France (where Celsius is used) that one cannot live with a temperature over 44 degrees. When the father explains to him the difference in scales, Schatz slowly relaxes, and the next day, "he cried very easily at little things that were of no importance."
Source (edited): "http://en.wikipedia.org/wiki/A_Day%27s_Wait"

# A Farewell to Arms

*A Farewell to Arms* is a semi-autobiographical novel written by Ernest Hemingway concerning events during the Italian campaigns during the First World War. The book, which was first published in 1929, is a first-person account of American Frederic Henry, serving as a Lieutenant ("Tenente") in the ambulance corps of the Italian Army. The title is taken from a poem by 16th-century English dramatist George Peele.

*A Farewell to Arms* works on two literary levels. Firstly it is a story concerning the drama and passion of a doomed romance between Henry and British nurse, Catherine Barkley. But secondly, it also skilfully contrasts the meaning of personal tragedy against the impersonal destruction wrought by the Great War. Hemingway deftly captures the cynicism of soldiers, the futility of war, and the displacement of populations. Although this was Hemingway's bleakest novel, its publication cemented his stature as a modern American writer.

In 1998, the Modern Library ranked *A Farewell to Arms* #74 on its list of the 100 best English-language novels of the 20th century. It was first adapted to film in 1932, with further versions in the following decades.

### Plot summary

The novel is divided into five books. In the first book, Rinaldi introduces Henry to Catherine Barkley; Henry attempts to seduce her, and their relationship begins. While on the Italian front, Henry is wounded in the knee by a mortar shell and sent to a hospital in Milan. The second book shows the growth of Henry and Catherine's relationship as they spend time together in Milan over the summer. Henry falls in love with Catherine and by the time he is healed, Catherine is three months pregnant. In the third book, Henry returns to his unit, but not long after, the Austro-Germans break through the Italian lines in the Battle of Caporetto, and the Italians retreat. Henry kills an engineering sergeant for insubordination. After falling behind and catching up again, Henry is taken to a place by the "battle police" where officers are being interrogated and executed for the "treachery" that supposedly led to the Italian defeat. However, after hearing the execution of a Lt.Colonel, Henry escapes by jumping into a river. In the fourth book, Catherine and Henry reunite and flee to Switzerland in a rowing boat. In the final book, Henry and Catherine live a quiet life in the mountains until she goes into labour. After a long and painful birth, their son is stillborn. Catherine begins to hemorrhage and soon dies, leaving Henry to return to their hotel in the rain.

### Characters

- **Frederic Henry**, often simply called **"Tenente"** ("Lieutenant"), is the narrator of the story. Henry is a volunteer ambulance driver from the United States. In Henry, we see the beginnings of what comes to be called Hemingway's "Code Hero": Henry is stoic under duress or pain; he modestly deflects praise for his contributions to the war; he is unflappable under fire; he does his work. He is a "man's man," in that his thoughts revolve on women ("girls") and drink. He participates in and seems to enjoy the banal, everyday conversation between the soldiers. He is attracted to the simple goodness of the priest, who, like Henry (who is not religious), sticks to his beliefs despite the war's constant presence. Henry is most characterized throughout the novel by his passionate love and dedication to Catherine Barkley.
- **Catherine Barkley** is a British Voluntary Aid Detachment Nurse. She loves the males so much that she started to write a short story about her love affairs with her fiance, who since has passed away. She volunteered in the war at the same time her fiance of eight years joined the army. He was killed in the Battle of the Somme. She is originally from Scotland, emotional, and dependent upon Henry's love for her. Her sexual desires and her simple desire for companionship are sometimes at odds with her needs to tend to the

ill. Like the code hero, she handles conflicting needs with grace, giving to both, but shorting none. Feminist thinkers will see in Catherine, Hemingway's perfect woman: wise and cynical in many ways, her wisdom cannot contain her desire. As Henry gives his health and youth to the war effort, Catherine's chief heroism is to accept the pain and death of childbirth stoically. Barkley has been "consistently ignored" as a code hero, probably because she is a woman.

- **Rinaldi** is a physician through whom Hemingway draws his idea of an Italian male. Sketched somewhat jingoistically, Rinaldi is unfailingly exuberant, ignoring small details that would stop his large and giving gestures. He loves women and alcohol, bearing a bottle of the latter and tales of the former to his friend Henry as Henry recovers from his wounds. He enjoys performing surgery, seeing it as an enjoyable challenge; he greets his friend Frederic Henry with a formal European-style kiss. He usually refers to Henry as "baby". Rinaldi is a form of the code hero as well. He allows Hemingway to explore another, non-Anglo-American, way of being male, of facing even a difficult world, an injured Italy, with joie de vivre, ignoring all danger, giving himself. Henry reunites with a tired and syphilitic Rinaldi in the middle of the novel, illustrating the flaws of this approach to the war and to life.
- **The Priest** The chaplain in Henry's unit. Baited by the other officers, he is befriended by Henry, to whom he offers spiritual advice. The last time we see this character, his faith is wavering. Can also be interpreted as a "Code Hero".
- **Helen Ferguson** Catherine's friend and fellow nurse, who expresses a strong distaste for Henry, because he impregnated her outside of marriage and during wartime. Hemingway based her on Kitty Cannell (1891 – 1974), an acquaintance of his who was a Paris-based American dance and fashion correspondent for major U.S. papers and periodicals.
- **Passini and Bonello** Ambulance drivers serving under Henry.
- **Manera, Gavuzzi, Gordini, Piani and Aymo** Other ambulance drivers.
- **Mrs. Walker** An American nurse at the American hospital in Milan.
- **Miss Gage** Another American nurse, sympathetic to Henry and Catherine's affair.
- **Miss Van Campen** The unsympathetic nursing superintendent at American Hospital in Milan.
- **Dr. Valentini** A surgeon who is highly competent and full of *joie de vivre*.
- **Meyers** A gloomy American expatriate.
- **Ettore Moretti** An Italian-American Officer from San Francisco serving in the Italian army.
- **Ralph Simmons** An American student of opera and Henry's friend.
- **Count Greffi** An old but vigorous Italian whom Henry knows from Stresa and who serves as a mentor to Henry.

## Censorship

In print, the words "shit", "fuck" and "cocksucker" were replaced with dashes ("----"). There are at least two copies of the first edition in which Hemingway re-inserted the censored text by hand, so as to provide a corrected text. One of these copies was presented to Maurice Coindreau; the other, to James Joyce. Hemingway's corrected text has not been incorporated into any published edition of the novel.

## Autobiographical details

The novel was based on Hemingway's own experiences serving in the Italian campaigns during the First World War. The inspiration for Catherine Barkley was Agnes von Kurowsky, a real nurse who cared for Hemingway in a hospital in Milan after he had been wounded. He had planned to marry her but she spurned his love when he returned to America. Kitty Cannell, a Paris-based fashion correspondent, became Helen Ferguson. The unnamed priest was based on Don Giuseppe Bianchi, the priest of the 69th and 70th regiments of the Brigata Ancona. Although the sources for Rinaldi are unknown, the character had already appeared in *In Our Time*.

## Publication history

The novel is believed to have been written at the home of Hemingway's in-laws in Piggott, Arkansas and at the home of friends of Hemingway's wife Pauline Pfeiffer W. Malcolm and Ruth Lowry home at 6435 Indian Lane, Mission Hills, Kansas while she was awaiting delivery of their baby. His wife Pauline underwent a caesarean section as Hemingway was writing about Catherine Barkley's childbirth.

The book was published at a time when many other World War I books were also appearing on the market. These included Frederic Manning's *Her Privates We*, Erich Maria Remarque's *All Quiet on the Western Front*, Richard Aldington's *Death of a Hero* and *Goodbye to All That* by Robert Graves. It was serialized in *Scribner's Magazine* from May 1929 to October 1929. The book was published in September 1929 with a first edition print-run of approximately 31,000 copies.

The success of *A Farewell to Arms* made Hemingway financially independent.

## Adaptations

- The novel was adapted for the stage by Laurence Stallings in 1930.
- The 1932 screen adaptation was nominated for the Academy Award for Best Picture. The screenplay was written by Oliver H.P. Garrett and Benjamin Glazer. It was directed by Frank Borzage and features the music of Richard Wagner. The movie stars Helen Hayes, Gary Cooper and Adolphe Menjou.
  - *A Farewell to Arms* was presented in five radio productions: December 1938 for CBS; during World War II for NBC; August 1948 for NBC; June 1949 for CBS; and October 1950 for NBC.

- A 1957 remake starring Rock Hudson, Jennifer Jones and Vittorio De Sica was directed by Charles Vidor and John Huston. De Sica was nominated for Best Supporting Actor for his performance.
- The BBC broadcast an abridged adaptation – written by Giles Cooper, directed by Rex Tucker and starring Vanessa Redgrave and George Hamilton – on February 15, 1966.
- The 1996 film *In Love and War*, starring Sandra Bullock and Chris O'Donnell, is loosely based on the novel. O'Donnell plays "Ernie", a Red Cross ambulance driver stationed in Italy during World War L

Source (edited): "http://en.wikipedia.org/wiki/A_Farewell_to_Arms"

# A Moveable Feast

*A Moveable Feast* is a set of memoirs by American author Ernest Hemingway (July 21, 1899 – July 2, 1961) about his years in Paris as part of the American expatriate circle of writers in the 1920s. The book describes Hemingway's apprenticeship as a young writer in Europe (especially in Paris) during the 1920s with his first wife, Hadley. Some of the later prominent people who are featured in his memoirs include Aleister Crowley, Ezra Pound, F. Scott Fitzgerald, Ford Madox Ford, Hilaire Belloc, Pascin, John Dos Passos, Wyndham Lewis, James Joyce and Gertrude Stein.

The book was not published during Hemingway's life, but edited from his manuscripts and notes by his widow and fourth wife, Mary Hemingway, a respected journalist. It was published in 1964, three years after Hemingway's death. An edition revised by his grandson Seán Hemingway (a descendant of Hemingway's second wife Pauline Pfeiffer and not a professional writer) was published in 2009. Both editions have been criticized.

The memoir consists of Hemingway's personal accounts, observations, and stories of his experience in 1920s Paris. He provides specific addresses of cafes, bars, hotels, and apartments, some of which can be found in modern-day Paris. The title was suggested by Hemingway's friend A.E. Hotchner, author of the biography, *Papa Hemingway*. He remembered they had a conversation about the city during Hotchner's first visits there: "If you are lucky enough to have lived in Paris as a young man, then wherever you go for the rest of your life, it stays with you, for Paris is a moveable feast."

## Background

In 1956 Hemingway found a trunk he had left years before in the basement of the Ritz Hotel in Paris. The trunk contained notebooks he had filled during the years he lived in Paris. He had the notebooks transcribed. During the period when he worked on the book, *The Dangerous Summer*, he also brought the Paris memoir to a final draft stage. Scribner's published *A Moveable Feast* in 1964 after Hemingway's death, when it had been edited by his fourth wife and widow, Mary Hemingway.

## Commentary on editing

Ernest Hemingway worked on the manuscript of *A Moveable Feast* during his later years, painstakingly rewriting several key passages. He had prepared a final draft before he died. After his death, his fourth wife Mary, in her capacity as Hemingway's literary executor, did editing in consultation with the publisher.

The contemporary literary scholar Gerry Brenner from the University of Montana documented her edits and questioned their validity in his 1982 paper, "Are We Going to Hemingway's Feast?". He concluded that some edits were misguided, and others derived from questionable motives. He suggested the changes appeared to contradict Mary's stated policy for her role as executor, which had been an avowed hands-off approach.

Brenner and other researchers have examined the collection of Ernest Hemingway's personal papers, which were opened to the public in 1979 with the completion of the John F. Kennedy Library, where they are held in Boston. Included are Hemingway's notes and initial drafts of *A Moveable Feast*. Brenner indicates that Mary changed the order of the chapters in Hemingway's final draft, apparently to "preserve chronology". Brenner notes he thought this change interrupted the series of juxtaposed character sketches of such individuals as Sylvia Beach (owner of the bookstore "Shakespeare and Company") and Gertrude Stein. Additionally, Brenner points out that one chapter, titled "Birth of a New School", which Hemingway had dropped in his draft, was re-inserted by Mary. He thought she did not have sufficient justification for its contents or execution.

Brenner alleges the most serious edit was deleting Hemingway's lengthy apology to Hadley, his first wife. This apology appeared in various forms in every draft of the book. Brenner suggests that Mary deleted it because it impugned her own role as wife.

In contrast, A.E. Hotchner has said that Mary Hemingway published essentially the draft which he had read in 1957. He believed it represented Ernest's intentions.

## New Edition

In 2009 a new edition, called the "Restored Edition," was published by Seán Hemingway, a grandson of Hemingway and his second wife Pauline Pfeiffer. He was an assistant curator at the Metropolitan Museum of Art. He made numerous changes:
- The previous introductory letter by Hemingway, pieced together from various fragments by Mary Hemingway, was removed.
- The chapter called "Birth of a New School" and large sections of "Ezra Pound and the Measuring Worm," "There is Never Any End to Paris," and "Winter in Schruns" have all

been re-added. The unpublished "The Pilot Fish and the Rich" has been added.
- Chapter 7 ("Shakespeare and Company") has been moved to be chapter 3, and chapter 16 ("Nada y Pues Nada") has been moved to the end of the book.
- Hemingway's use of the second person has been restored in many places, a change which Seán asserts "brings the reader into the story."

From the new foreword by Patrick Hemingway:
[H]ere is the last bit of professional writing by my father, the true foreword to *A Moveable Feast*: "This book contains material from the *remises* of my memory and of my heart. Even if the one has been tampered with and the other does not exist."

**Criticism**

A.E. Hotchner, a friend and biographer of Hemingway, alleged that Seán Hemingway had edited the new edition, in part, to exclude references to his grandmother, Hemingway's second wife Pauline Pfeiffer, which he had found less than flattering. Other critics also have found fault with some of the editorial changes. Irene Gammel writes about the new edition: "Ethically and pragmatically, restoring an author's original intent is a slippery slope when the published text has stood the test of time and when edits have been approved by authors or their legal representatives." Pointing to the complexity of the author-function, she concludes: "Mary's version should be considered the definitive one, while the 'restored' version provides access to important unpublished contextual sources that illuminate the evolution of the 1964 edition."

**Implications of sexual identity and androgyny**

In discussion of other issues related to the memoir, the literary critic J. Gerald Kennedy of Louisiana State University pointed out the artificially heroic nature of Hemingway's self-portrait in *A Moveable Feast*. He contrasted it with the sexual ambiguity and fascination with androgyny found in Hemingway's unfinished novel, *The Garden of Eden*. Kennedy examines how textual evidence from both published material and unpublished papers from the collection at the JFK Library seem to project a contrasting picture of Hemingway's sexuality. Noting that the clumsy "created" nature of the young Hemingway in *A Moveable Feast* is well-established as fraudulent (e.g., Hemingway had access to large sums of money during the time he was in Paris, yet portrayed himself as "starving"), Kennedy points out that Hemingway writes as if he were the only person in his literary circle in Paris who was sexually stable and healthy, in contrast to F. Scott Fitzgerald and Gertrude Stein. This self-assured image, however, is in stark contrast with the confused and experimenting protagonist of *The Garden of Eden*.

Kennedy notes significant textual clues, such as a fascination with androgynous haircuts and the redacted sections of *A Moveable Feast*, which refer to the period when Hemingway was having an affair with his second wife Pauline while still married to Hadley. Kennedy concluded Hemingway's "obsession" with indistinct gendering was central to his character, a conclusion also alleged by the critic Mark Spilka and biographer Kenneth Lynn.

**Film and television adaptations**

On September 15, 2009, *Daily Variety* announced that Mariel Hemingway, a granddaughter of Ernest Hemingway and first wife Hadley Richardson, had acquired the film and television rights to the memoir with American film producer John Goldstone.
Source (edited): "http://en.wikipedia.org/wiki/A_Moveable_Feast"

# A Simple Enquiry

**A Simple Enquiry** is a short story written by Ernest Hemingway. It was published in 1927 in the collection *Men Without Women*.

**Synopsis**

A major calls his 19-year old orderly into his room and questions him about his personal life. He appears to be propositioning the orderly, and when his advances are effectively rebuffed he dismisses the orderly from the room, with the understanding that he will not press the issue.

**Characters**
- The major
- Tomani, an adjutant
- Pinin, the major's orderly

Source (edited): "http://en.wikipedia.org/wiki/A_Simple_Enquiry"

# A Very Short Story

"**A Very Short Story**" is a short story written by Ernest Hemingway. It was first published in 1925 in the short story collection *In Our Time*.

## Synopsis

Ernest Hemingway's relationship with Agnes von Kurowsky was the basis for this story.

A World War I soldier and a nurse named "Luz" fall in love as she tends to him over the course of three months in the hospital. They agree to get married, but after the soldier returns home to the United States, Luz writes to him that she has fallen in love with an officer. Later she writes that she hasn't gotten married, but the soldier ignores her. The soldier contracts "the clap" from a casual encounter, shortly afterward.

Hemingway's first serious relationship with Agnes von Kurowsky, a nurse he met while recuperating from his WWI injuries, was the basis for this story.
Source (edited): "http://en.wikipedia.org/wiki/A_Very_Short_Story"

# Across the River and into the Trees

*Across the River and Into the Trees* is a novel by American writer Ernest Hemingway, published by Charles Scribner's Sons in September 1950. Prior to publication the novel was serialized in Cosmopolitan Magazine. The title is derived from the last words of Confederate General Thomas J. (Stonewall) Jackson.

The opening of the novel is set in Trieste, on the last day in the life of the protagonist, Colonel Cantwell. Much of the novel is a protracted flashback, during which Cantwell reminisces about a young Venetian woman, Renata, and his life as a soldier during the war.

An important theme in the novel is that of death and how one faces death. One biographer and critic sees a parallel between Hemingway's *Across the River and Into the Trees* and Thomas Mann's *Death in Venice*. Generally critics agree the novel is built upon successive layers of symbolism. As in his other writing, Hemingway employs the style known as the iceberg theory in which much of the substance of the work lies below the surface of the plot itself.

The novel was written in Italy, Cuba and France. While visiting Italy, Hemingway met a young woman with whom he had a protracted relationship which has been defined as a father-daughter relationship. The woman, Adriana Ivancich, became the model for the female character in the novel.

With some exceptions, *Across the River and Into the Trees* received bad reviews, and was the first of his novels to receive consistently bad press. In the years since its publication, however, some critics have come to believe it is an important addition to the Hemingway canon.

### Plot summary

*Across the River and Into the Trees* begins in the first chapter with the frame story of 50-year-old Colonel Cantwell's duckhunting trip to Trieste set in time-present. In the second chapter, Hemingway moves Cantwell back in time with a stream of consciousness interior monologue, presenting an extended flashback and continues for 38 chapters. In the final six chapters Cantwell is presented again in the frame-story set in the time-present.

Cantwell, who is dying of heart disease, spends a Sunday afternoon in a duck blind in Trieste. In the flashback he thinks of his recent weekend in Venice with 18-year-old Renata, moving backward in time to ruminate about his experiences during the war. The novel ends with Cantwell suffering a series of fatal heart attacks as he leaves the duck blind.

## Themes

Hemingway biographer and scholar Carlos Baker writes in *Hemingway: The Writer as Artist* that in *Across the River and Into the Trees* the overriding theme is that of "the three ages of man." Furthermore, Baker considers the writing of the book a necessity for Hemingway to objectify his war experiences. Jeffrey Meyers, author of *Hemingway: A Biography*, believes Hemingway saw Adriana as a representation of Venice, that she "connected" him to Italy, and that theirs was a type of father-daughter relationship which Hemingway romanticized. As she appears in the novel, Renata is physically the same as Adriana, and Baker presents the probability that Hemingway used Cantwell's fictional relationship with Renata as a substitute for his own relationship with Adriana.

Baker sees a thematic parallel between Thomas Mann's *Death in Venice* and *Across the River and into the Trees*, presented via a series of commonalities and differences. *Death in Venice* is set in the summer on the Lido; Hemingway places Cantwell in Venice in the winter. Mann's protagonist is a writer; Hemingway's a soldier. Both face death, and in the face of death seek solace in a much younger character. Cantwell reminisces about the past while Renata (the 18 year-old countess with whom he spends his final days) focuses on the present. According to Cantwell "Every day is a new and fine illusion" in which always lies a kernel of truth. Baker considers Cantwell as a character with opposing qualities: he is a tough soldier and he is a tender friend and lover. The two Cantwells are juxtaposed and at times overlap and bleed into one another. Moreover, Baker explains that Hemingway added yet another layer in which the 50-year-old Cantwell of 1950 is "in an intense state of awareness" of the young Cantwell of 1918: they are the same character yet different.

Charles Oliver, author of *Ernest Hemingway A to Z: The Essential Reference to the Life and Work*, writes that the novel shows a common Hemingway theme of "maintaining control over one's life, even in the face of terrible odds." Cantwell knows he is dying and faces death "with the dignity which he believes he has maintained throughout his military service." The theme of death is central in Hemingway's writings and Stoltzfus argues that in Hemingway's fictional characters achieve redemption at the moment of death if death is faced with authenticity which is a form of existentialism. Jean-Paul Sartre believed the "clue to facing life" was death. Therefore to face death well, is to live a heightened existence.

Jackson Benson believes Hemingway used autobiographical details to work as framing devices to write about life in general—not only about his life. For example, Benson postulates that Hemingway used his experiences and drew them out further with "what if" scenarios: "what if I were wounded in such a way that I could not sleep at night? What if I were wounded and made crazy, what would happen if I were sent back to the front?" In "Ernest Hemingway: The Life as Fiction and the Fiction as Life" Benson argues that critics must ignore finding connections between the author's life and fiction and instead focus on the manner in which biographical events are transformed into art. He believes the events in a writer's life might have only a "very tenuous relationship" to the fiction in the manner of a dream from which a drama emerges. Hemingway's later fiction, Benson writes "is like an adolescent day-dream in which he acts out infatuation and consumation, as in *Across the River*." Meyers agrees that parallels exist between Hemingway and Colonel Cantwell, but he sees more similarities with Hemingway's friend of many decades "Chink" Dorman-Smith whose military career was undermined resulting in his demotion.

## Writing style and genre

Hemingway began as a writer of short stories, and as Baker explains, he learned how to "get the most from the least, how to prune language how to multiply intensities, and how to tell nothing but the truth in a way that allowed for telling more than the truth". The style is known as the Iceberg Theory because in Hemingway's writing the hard facts float above water; the supporting structure, complete with symbolism, operates out-of-sight. The concept of the iceberg theory is sometimes referred to as the "theory of omission." Hemingway believed the writer could describe one thing though an entirely different thing occurs below the surface. Baker calls *Across the River and into the Trees* a "lyric-poetical novel" in which each scene has an underlying truth presented via symbolism. According to Meyers an example of omission is that Renata, like other heroines in Hemingway's fiction, suffers a major "shock"—the murder of her father and the subsequent loss of her home—to which Hemingway alludes only briefly. Hemingway's pared down narrative forces the reader to solve connections. As Stoltzfus remarks: "Hemingway walks the reader to the bridge that he or she must cross alone without the narrator's help."

Hemingway constructed *Across the River and into the Trees* to allow time to be compressed in the novel such that "memory and space-time coalesce." For example, to move Cantwell into the extended flashback Hemingway uses the word "boy" to bridge time-present with time-past. Stoltzfus points out Hemingway kept the dialogue in the present tense, despite the time-shifts, and to "reinforce the illusion" he repeatedly used the word "now".

## Development and background

Ernest Hemingway met his friend A. E. Hotchner in 1948 when Hotchner, recently released from the Air Force, took a job with *Cosmopolitan Magazine* as a "commissioned agent." Hemingway's name was on the list of authors Hotchner was to contact so he went to Cuba, asked for a meeting (Hemingway took him to a bar) and for a short article. Hemingway did not write an article, but he did submit his next novel *Across the River and into the Trees* to Hotchner which *Cosmopolitan* serialized in five installments.

From 1949 to 1950 Hemingway

worked on the book in four different places: he started writing during the winter of 1949 in Italy at Cortina D'Ampezzo; continued upon his return home to Cuba; finished the draft in Paris; and completed the revisions in Venice in the winter of 1950. In the fall of 1948 he arrived in Italy and visited Fossalta where in 1918 he had been wounded. A month later, while duck hunting with an Italian aristocrat he met 18-year-old Adriana Ivancich. He and his fourth wife Mary then went to Cortina to ski: she broke her ankle and, bored, Hemingway began the draft of the book. Hemingway himself then became ill with an eye-infection and was hospitalized. In the spring he went to Venice where he met Adriana for lunch a few times. In May he returned to Cuba and carried out a protracted correspondence with Adriana while working on the manuscript. In the autumn he had returned to Europe and at the Ritz in Paris he finished the draft. Once done, he and Mary went again to Cortina to ski: for the second time she broke her ankle and he contracted an eye infection. By February the first serialization was published in *Cosmopolitan* and in March the Hemingways returned to Paris and then home to Cuba where the final proofs were read before the September publication.

## Reception

John O'Hara wrote in the *New York Times*; "The most important author living today, the outstanding author since the death of Shakespeare, has brought out a new novel. The title of the novel is *Across the River and Into the Trees*." The author, of course, is Ernest Hemingway, the most important, the outstanding author out of the millions of writers who have lived since 1616." However, O'Hara's was one the few good reviews, with negative reviews appearing in more than 150 publications. Critics claimed the novel was too emotional had inferior prose and a "static plot", and that Cantwell was an "avatar" for Hemingway's character Nick Adams. The novel was criticized for being an unsuitable autobiography, and for presenting Cantwell as a bitter soldier.

Tennessee Williams, in *The New York Times*, wrote: "I could not go to Venice, now, without hearing the haunted cadences of Hemingway's new novel. It is the saddest novel in the world about the saddest city, and when I say I think it is the best and most honest work that Hemingway has done, you may think me crazy. It will probably be a popular book. The critics may treat it pretty roughly. But its hauntingly tired cadences are the direct speech of a man's heart who is speaking that directly for the first time, and that makes it, for me, the finest thing Hemingway has done."
—Ernest Hemingway about critical reception to *Across the River and into the Trees*.

According to Baker, Hemingway was "deeply wounded by the negative reviews" of this novel. Furthermore, Baker explains Hemingway was unaware that those close to him agreed with the majority of critics. For example, his wife Mary, who disapproved of *Across the River and into the Trees*, said: "I kept my mouth shut. Nobody had appointed me my husband's editor."

Generally the novel is considered better than the critical reviews received upon publication. Baker compares it to Shakespeare's *Winter's Tale* or *The Tempest*: not a major work, but one with an 'elegiac" tone. Meyers believes the novel shows a new "confessional mode" in Hemingway's work and that it "would have been hailed as more impressive if it had been written by anyone but Hemingway." Stoltzfus agrees, and he believes Hemingway's structure is more comprehensible for the modern reader—exposed to the Nouveau roman—than for those of the mid-20th century.

## Publication history

*Cosmopolitan Magazine* serialized *Across the River and Into the Woods* from February to June 1950. Adriana Ivancich designed the dustjacket of the first edition, although her original artwork was redrawn by the Scribner's promotions department. The novel was published by Scribner's on 7 September 1950 with a first edition print run of 75,000, after a publicity campaign that hailed the novel as Hemingway's first book since the publication of his 1940 Spanish Civil War novel *For Whom the Bell Tolls*.

Source (edited): "http://en.wikipedia.org/wiki/Across_the_River_and_into_the_Trees"

# Big Two-Hearted River

"**Big Two-Hearted River**" is a two-part short story written by American author Ernest Hemingway published in 1925 in his first collection of stories, *In Our Time*.

The story is generally viewed as an account of a healing process for Nick Adams, recently returned from WWI. In the story, Nick returns to his boyhood activities of camping and fishing. Hemingway use of the theory of omission allows him to present Nick's camping trip while the crux of the story is Nick's return to nature to heal from the devastation of war, which is never explicitly stated.

## Plot summary

As Nick hikes through a burned-out forest he notices grasshoppers that have turned black from the effects of the fire which burned down the town, as well as the passivity of the trout in the river, resting in the current rather than fighting upstream. Nick also realizes, upon stepping off the train in Seney, and seeing the "burned-over stretch of hillside", that he himself has changed just as much as the land has.

Once Nick finds a suitable campsite, he distracts himself by meticulously pitching his tent and cooking dinner. Hemingway's prose reflects this distraction by outlining in detail every one of Nick's actions rather than his thoughts. Before he goes to bed, Nick thinks about a friend of his, and the way that he used to make coffee, smiling at the memories. He goes to bed happy, anticipating a day of fishing.

The second part of the story begins as Nick wakes up in the morning, anxious to begin fishing. He makes flapjacks for breakfast and goes to find grasshoppers for bait. As Nick's activity begins to revolve around his interactions with nature, i.e., the grasshoppers and the trout, a change begins to occur in the text itself, coming alive with Nick's continually stabilizing condition. No longer is he fixated on the negative passivity of his situation, the helplessness and hopelessness he experienced in the war. Now he is engaged in his surroundings, doing something, rather than watching things happen around him.

Nick catches a small fish, and releases it, knowing that larger fish are to be had. Soon, he strikes a big fish:

"There was a long tug. Nick struck and the rod came alive and dangerous, bent double, the line tightening, coming out of the water, tightening, all in a heavy, dangerous, steady pull. Nick felt the moment when the leader would break if the strain increased and let the line go."

After the big fish gets away, Nick proceeds to catch two medium-sized fish and is satisfied with them. He begins to lose interest in fishing and wishes instead that he had a book to read. Eventually, he notices a swamp upstream and thinks about the complications of fishing in it. Nick resolves not to try to fish in the swamp.

## The River

The Two Hearted River is situated in Michigan's Upper Peninsula and empties into Lake Superior. Hemingway fans, fishermen, and canoers occasionally rent canoes, during the summer, for a trip downstream to the lake. However, the geography in the story indicates that the river in the story was actually the Fox River, which flows through Seney and into Lake Michigan. Hemingway admitted to changing the name used in the story because Two Hearted was more poetic.

The biggest local hazards are the black flies, which inflict painful bites. During the winter, the area tends to become impassable except by snowmobile. By the mid 1960s, the forest, which had been logged-over before Hemingway's last visit, was beginning to recover. An occasional large tree, left behind to repopulate the forest, could be found, along with a larger number of smaller trees with a two to four inch trunk diameter.

Source (edited): "http://en.wikipedia.org/wiki/Big_Two-Hearted_River"

# Cat in the Rain

"Cat in the Rain" is a short story by Ernest Hemingway, written while the author was living in France. It was first published in 1925 in the short story collection *In Our Time*.

It is about an American couple on vacation in Italy. While at their hotel the woman sees a cat and the story progresses from there. During the story it is made obvious that the couple's relationship is going sour. Hemingway uses the cat stuck in the rain with nobody to care for it to symbolize the wife who longs to be loved. Hemingway claims in a letter to F. Scott Fitzgerald that the story was not about his marriage to his first wife, which was falling apart at the same time the story was written.

For a linguistic analysis focused on the relationship between the use of grammatical features (such as nominal group structure and modality), see Carter (1982).

Source (edited): "http://en.wikipedia.org/wiki/Cat_in_the_Rain"

# *Dateline: Toronto*

*Dateline: Toronto* is a collection of most of the stories that Ernest Hemingway wrote as a stringer and later staff writer and foreign correspondent for the *Toronto Star* between 1920 and 1924. The stories were written while Hemingway was in his early 20s before he became well-known, and show his development as a writer. The collection was edited by William White, a professor of English literature and journalism at Wayne State University, and a regular contributor to The Hemingway Review.

## Background

In 1920, after returning from World War I, Hemingway moved to Toronto where he began freelancing for the *Toronto Star Weekly*, part of the *Toronto Star*. For his earliest work, Hemingway was paid $5 and eventually hired by the paper. On March 6, 1920, Ernest M. Hemingway received his first byline for the Toronto Star Weekly, a story entitled "Taking a Chance for a Free Shave." The story was about a trip to a barber college, where shaves were free, but performed by inexperienced barbers still in training.

Hemingway continued writing features at a rate of about one a week. He stayed in Toronto off and on for two years, earning about $45 a week. During this time he wrote stories on a wide array of subjects — from the benefits of centralized government purchasing ("Buying Commission Would Cut Out Waste", *The Toronto Daily Star*, April 26, 1920) to a boxing match between Georges Carpentier and Jack Dempsey ("Carpentier Sure to Give Dempsey Fight Worth While", *The Toronto Star Weekly*, October 30, 1920) to a humorous look at returning World War I veterans ("Lieutenants' Mustaches the Only Permanent Thing We Got Out of War", *The Toronto Star Weekly*, April 10, 1920.)

In 1921 Hemingway returned to Chicago and wrote dispatches from there. In December 1921, Hemingway's career changed forever when he went to Europe with his wife and as a foreign correspondent wrote human-interest stories about post-war conditions. Here he made his first experience of bull-fighting, the sport that came to be so important in his writings.

After much success as a foreign correspondent, Hemingway returned to Toronto in 1923. But upon his return, Hemingway had a bitter falling out with his editor, Harry Hindmarsh, who believed Hemingway had been spoiled by his time overseas. Hindmarsh gave Hemingway mundane assignments, and Hemingway grew bitter and wrote an angry resignation in December 1923. Even his resignation was ignored, and Hemingway continued to write sporadically through 1924. In 1924, Hemingway published *in our time* (in lower case) which was the foundation for *In Our Time*, and Hemingway decided to leave the Star.

### *Dateline: Toronto*

The collection *Dateline: Toronto* contains 172 articles that Hemingway wrote for the Star. At the time of the collection's publication, in 1985, it was believed to contain the complete works of Ernest Hemingway for the Star.

Determining which stories Hemingway wrote, however, was not a straightforward task. In the 1920s, it was common for newspaper stories to run without crediting the author. Of the stories in the collection, only 137 were bylined Ernest M. Hemingway (Hemingway did not stop using his middle initial until later in his career). The rest of the stories had either no byline, or occasionally pseudonyms if Hemingway already had one story in the paper.

In researching Hemingway's career for the Centennial of the *Toronto Star*, reporter William Burrill uncovered evidence of 30 additional stories that Hemingway had written for the *Toronto Star*, but had been either missed by earlier researchers, published without Hemingway's bylines, or published under such bylines as "Peter Jackson" or "John Hadley", which were known Hemingway pseudonyms already identified in White's collection When Hemingway had returned from Europe, his editor possibly punished him by refusing to allow him bylines, but many of the stories identified by Burrill had evidence pointing to Hemingway's authorship. (Most of these additional "lost" stories can be found in William Burrill's book "Hemingway, The Toronto Years" a 392-page award-winning biography that also fully reprints 25 of the "lost" Hemingway stories in Burrill's 135-page Appendix. (Doubleday Canada, Hardcover 1994, ISBN 0-385-25489-X and Trade Paper 1995, ISBN 0-385-25558-6). Furthermore, Burrill points out that the *Toronto Star* archives only maintained copies of the final edition of the newspaper; Hemingway may have written stories that fell out of the final edition and as such his complete works for the Toronto Star may never be known.

### Hemingway style

Many of the stylistic techniques and themes that would characterize Hemingway's writing were first put to use for the *Star*. In a dispatch from Spain in 1922 Hemingway would write a passage reminiscent of his Pulitzer-prize winning The Old Man and the Sea:

But if you land a big tuna after a six-hour fight, fight him man against fish until your muscles are nauseated with the unceasing strain, and finally bring him up alongside the boat, green-blue and silver in the lazy ocean, you will be purified and will be able to enter unabashed into the presence of the very elder gods and they will make you welcome." Ideas later surfaced in The Old Man and the Sea. "At Vigo, in Spain, Is Where You Catch the Silver and Blue Tuna, the King of All Fish, *The Toronto Star Weekly*, February 18, 1922

On assignment for the *Toronto Star*, Hemingway also wrote about his first bullfight in a lengthy feature ("Bull-Fighting Is Not a Sport--It Is a Tragedy", *The Toronto Star Weekly*, October 20, 1923). Bullfighting would become a major motif in Hemingway's writing, appearing in *The Sun Also Rises* and *Death in the Afternoon*. Hemingway's stories also displayed his characteristic sparse use of language, attention to detail, and ear for dialogue.

A humorous streak is also present in much of Hemingway's newspaper writing. Humor, however was not common in Hemingway's later writing, possibly because the humor reminded him of journalism, or because he believed the humor was simply not appropriate in serious literature. All the literary and humorous flourishes in Hemingway's writing have led to suspicion that Hemingway's stories may have included details that were embellished.

Hemingway himself would grow to disavow his newspaper writing, and did not wish for it to be compared to his later publications. Hemingway reportedly would become infuriated at such comparisons.

Source (edited): "http://en.wikipedia.org/wiki/Dateline:_Toronto"

# *Death in the Afternoon*

*Death in the Afternoon* is a non-fiction book by Ernest Hemingway (July 21, 1899 – July 2, 1961) about the ceremony and traditions of Spanish bullfighting. It was originally published in 1932.

The book provides a look at the history and what Hemingway considers the magnificence of bullfighting. It also contains a deeper contemplation on the nature of fear and courage.

Any discussion concerning bullfighting would be incomplete without some mention of the controversy surrounding it. Toward that end Hemingway commented, "anything capable of arousing passion in its favor will surely raise as much passion against it."

Walkway named for Ernest Hemingway, Ronda, Spain

Hemingway became a bullfighting aficionado after seeing the Pamplona fiesta in the 1920s, which he wrote about in *The Sun Also Rises*. In *Death in the Afternoon*, Hemingway explores the metaphysics of bullfighting—the ritualized, almost religious practice—that he considered analgous to the writer's search for meaning and the essence of life. In bullfighting, he found the elemental nature of life and death. In his writings on Spain, he was influenced by the Spanish master Pío Baroja. When Hemingway won the Nobel Prize, he traveled to see Baroja, then on his death bed, specifically to tell him he thought Baroja deserved the prize more than he. Baroja agreed and something of the usual Hemingway tiff with another writer ensued despite his original good intentions.

*Death in the Afternoon* was published by Scribner's on 23 September 1932 to a first edition print run of approximately 10,000 copies.

"Death in the Afternoon" also refers to a cocktail invented by Hemingway: "Pour one jigger absinthe into a Champagne glass. Add iced Champagne until it attains the proper opalescent milkiness. Drink three to five of these slowly." It first appeared in a 1935 collection of cocktail recipes by famous authors of the time, edited by Sterling North and Carl Kroch: *So Red the Nose, or, Breath in the Afternoon*.

Wolcott Gibbs satirized the story and much of Hemingway's work in *The New Yorker* with his parody "Death in the Rumble Seat."

Source (edited): "http://en.wikipedia.org/wiki/Death_in_the_Afternoon"

# Ernest Hemingway

**Ernest Miller Hemingway** (July 21, 1899 – July 2, 1961) was an American author and journalist. His distinctive writing style, characterized by economy and understatement, influenced 20th-century fiction, as did his life of adventure and public image. He produced most of his work between the mid-1920s and the mid-1950s. He won the Nobel Prize in Literature in 1954. Hemingway's fiction was successful because the characters he presented exhibited authenticity that resonated with his audience. Many of his works are classics of American literature. He published seven novels, six short story collections, and two non-fiction works during his lifetime; a further three novels, four collections of short stories, and three non-fiction works were published posthumously.

Hemingway was born and raised in Oak Park, Illinois. After leaving high school he worked for a few months as a reporter for *The Kansas City Star*, before leaving for the Italian front to become an ambulance driver during World War I, which became the basis for his novel *A Farewell to Arms*. He was seriously wounded and returned home within the year. In 1922 Hemingway married Hadley Richardson, the first of his four wives, and the couple moved to Paris, where he worked as a foreign correspondent. During his time there he met and was influenced by modernist writers and artists of the 1920s expatriate community known as the "Lost Generation". His first novel, *The Sun Also Rises*, was published in 1926.

After divorcing Hadley Richardson in 1927 Hemingway married Pauline Pfeiffer; they divorced following Hemingway's return from covering the Spanish Civil War, after which he wrote *For Whom the Bell Tolls*. Martha Gellhorn became his third wife in 1940, but he left her for Mary Welsh after World War II, during which he was present at D-Day and the liberation of Paris.

Shortly after the publication of *The Old Man and the Sea* in 1952 Hemingway went on safari to Africa, where he was almost killed in a plane crash that left him in pain or ill-health for much of the rest of his life. Hemingway had permanent residences in Key West, Florida, and Cuba during the 1930s and '40s, but in 1959 he moved from Cuba to Ketchum, Idaho, where he committed suicide in the summer of 1961.

## Biography

### Early life

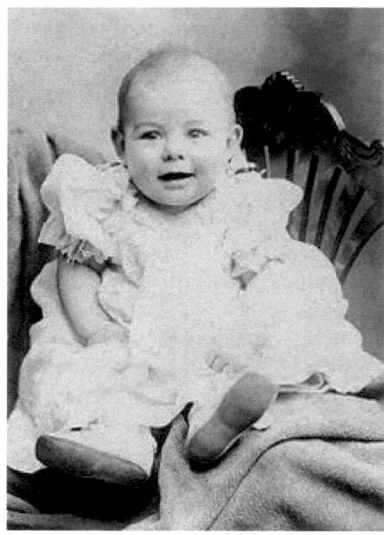

Ernest Hemingway was the second child, and first son, born to Clarence and Grace Hemingway.

Ernest Miller Hemingway was born on July 21, 1899, in Oak Park, Illinois, a suburb of Chicago. His father Clarence Edmonds Hemingway was a physician, and his mother, Grace Hall-Hemingway, was a musician. Both were well educated and well respected in the conservative community of Oak Park. Frank Lloyd Wright, a resident of Oak Park, said of the village: "So many churches for so many good people to go to". When Clarence and Grace Hemingway married in 1896, they moved in with Grace's father, Ernest Hall, after whom they named their first son. Hemingway claimed to dislike his name, which he "associated with the naive, even foolish hero of Oscar Wilde's play *The Importance of Being Earnest*". The family's seven-bedroom home in a respectable neighborhood contained a music studio for Grace and a medical office for Clarence.

Hemingway's mother frequently performed in concerts around the village. As an adult Hemingway professed to hate his mother, although biographer Michael Reynolds points out that Hemingway mirrored her energy and enthusiasm. Her insistence that he learn to play the cello became a "source of conflict", but he later admitted the music lessons were useful in his writing, as in the "contrapunctal structure" of *For Whom the Bell Tolls*. The family owned a summer home called Windemere on Walloon Lake, near Petoskey, Michigan, where Hemingway learned to hunt, fish and camp in the woods and lakes of Northern Michigan. His early experiences in nature instilled a passion for outdoor adventure, and living in remote or isolated areas.

Photograph of Hemingway family in 1905, from left: Marcelline, Sunny, Clarence, Grace, Ursula and Ernest.

Hemingway attended Oak Park and River Forest High School from 1913 until 1917 where he took part in a number of sports—boxing, track and field, water polo, and football—had good grades in English classes, and he and his sister Marcelline performed in the school orchestra for two years. In his junior year, he took a journalism class, taught by Fannie Biggs, which was structured "as though the classroom were a newspaper office". The better writers in class submitted pieces to the *The Trapeze*, the school newspaper. Hemingway and his sister Marcelline both had pieces submitted to *The Trapeze*; Hemingway's first piece, published in January 1916, was about a local performance by the Chicago Symphony Orchestra. He continued to contribute to and to edit the *Trapeze* and the *Tabula* (the school's newspaper and yearbook), for which he imitated the language of sportswriters, and used the pen name Ring Lardner, Jr.—a nod to Ring Lardner of the *Chicago Tribune* whose byline was "Line O'Type". Like Mark Twain, Stephen Crane, Theodore Dreiser and Sinclair Lewis, Hemingway was a journalist before becoming a novelist; after leaving high school he went to work for *The Kansas City Star* as a cub reporter. Although he stayed there for only six months he relied on the *Star's* style guide as a foundation for his writing: "Use short sentences. Use short first paragraphs. Use vigorous English. Be positive, not negative."

## World War I

Hemingway photographed in Milan, 1918, dressed in uniform. For two months he drove ambulances until he was wounded.

Early in 1918 Hemingway responded to a Red Cross recruitment effort and signed on to be an ambulance driver in Italy. He left New York in May, and arrived in Paris as the city was under bombardment from German artillery. By June he was stationed at the Italian Front, and on his first day in Milan was sent to the scene of a munitions factory explosion where rescuers retrieved the shredded remains of female workers. He described the incident in his nonfiction book *Death in the Afternoon*: "I remember that after we searched quite thoroughly for the complete dead we collected fragments". A few days later he was stationed at Fossalta di Piave. On July 8 he was seriously wounded by mortar fire, having just returned from the canteen to deliver chocolate and cigarettes to the men at the front line. Despite his wounds, Hemingway carried an Italian soldier to safety, for which he received the Italian Silver Medal of Bravery. Still only eighteen, Hemingway said of the incident: "When you go to war as a boy you have a great illusion of immortality. Other people get killed; not you ... Then when you are badly wounded the first time you lose that illusion and you know it can happen to you." He sustained shrapnel wounds to both legs; underwent an operation at a distribution center; spent five days at a field hospital; and was transferred to the Red Cross hospital in Milan for recuperation. Hemingway spent six months in the hospital, where he met and fell in love with Agnes von Kurowsky, a Red Cross nurse seven years his senior. Agnes and Hemingway planned to marry, but she became engaged to an Italian officer in March 1919, an incident that provided material for the short and bitter work "A Very Short Story". Biographer Jeffrey Meyers claims Hemingway was devastated by Agnes' rejection, and that he followed a pattern of abandoning a wife before she abandoned him in future relationships. During his six months in recuperation Hemingway met and formed a strong friendship with "Chink" Dorman-Smith that lasted for decades.

**Toronto and Chicago**
Hemingway returned home early in 1919 to a time of readjustment. At not yet 20 years old, the war had created in him a maturity at odds with living at home without a job and the need for recuperation. As Reynolds explains, "Hemingway could not really tell his parents what he thought when he saw his bloody knee. He could not say how scared he was in another country with surgeons who could not tell him in English if his leg was coming off or not." That summer he spent time in Michigan with high school friends, fishing and camping; and in September he spent a week in the back-country. The trip became the inspiration for his short story "Big Two-Hearted River", in which the semi-autobiographical character Nick Adams takes to the country to find solitude after returning from war. A family friend offered him a job in Toronto; having nothing else to do he accepted. Late that year he began as a freelancer, staff writer and foreign correspondent for the *Toronto Star Weekly*. However he returned to Michigan the following June, and then moved to Chicago in September 1920 to live with friends, while still filing stories for the *Toronto Star*.

In Chicago he worked as an associate editor of the monthly journal *Cooperative Commonwealth*, where he met Sherwood Anderson. When St. Louis native Hadley Richardson came to Chicago to visit Hemingway's roommate's sister, Hemingway, who was infatuated, later claimed "I knew she was the girl I was going to marry". Hadley was red-haired, with a "nurturing instinct", and eight years older than Hemingway. Despite the difference in age, Hadley, who had an overprotective mother, seemed less mature than usual for a young woman her age. Bernice Kert, author of *The Hemingway Women*, claims Hadley was "evocative" of Agnes, but that Hadley had a childishness that Agnes lacked. The two corresponded for a few months, and then decided to marry and travel to Europe. They wanted to visit Rome, but Sherwood Anderson convinced them to visit Paris instead. They were married on September 3, 1921; two months later Hemingway was hired as foreign correspondent for the *Toronto Star*; and the couple left for Paris. Of Hemingway's marriage to Hadley, Meyers claims: "With Hadley, Hemingway achieved everything he had hoped for with Agnes: the love of a beautiful woman, a comfortable income, a life in Europe."

**Paris**

Hemingway's 1923 passport photo. At this time he lived in Paris with his wife Hadley, and worked as a journalist.

Early Hemingway biographer Carlos Baker believes that, while Anderson suggested Paris because "the monetary exchange rate" made it an inexpensive place to live, more importantly it was where "the most interesting people in the world" resided. There Hemingway would meet writers such as Gertrude Stein, James Joyce and Ezra Pound who "could help a young writer up the rungs of a career". The Hemingway of the early Paris years was a "tall, handsome, muscular, broad-shouldered, brown-eyed, rosy-cheeked, square-jawed, soft-voiced young man." He and Hadley lived in a small walk-up at 74 Rue du Cardinal Lemoine in the Latin Quarter, and he worked in a rented room in a nearby building. Anderson wrote letters of introduction to Gertrude Stein and other writers in Paris. Stein, who was the bastion of modernism in Paris, became Hemingway's mentor for a period, introducing him to the expatriate artists and writers of the Montparnasse Quarter. She referred to artists as the "Lost Generation"—a term Hemingway popularized with the publication of *The Sun Also Rises*. A regular at Stein's salon, Hemingway met influential painters such as Pablo Picasso, Joan Miró, and Juan Gris. However, Hemingway eventually withdrew from Stein's influence and their relationship deteriorated into a literary quarrel that spanned decades. The American poet Ezra Pound, older than Hemingway by 14 years, met Hemingway by chance at Sylvia Beach's Shakespeare and Company in 1922. The two toured Italy in 1923 and lived on the same street in 1924. They forged a strong friendship and in Hemingway, Pound recognized and fostered a young talent. Pound—who had recently finished editing T. S. Eliot's *The Waste Land*—introduced Hemingway to the Irish writer James Joyce, with whom Hemingway frequently embarked on "alcoholic sprees".

Ernest Hemingway with Lady Duff Twysden, Hadley Hemingway, and three unidentified people at a cafe in Pamplona, Spain, July 1925

During his first 20 months in Paris, Hemingway filed 88 stories for the *Toronto Star*. He covered the Greco-Turkish War, where he witnessed the burning of Smyrna; wrote travel pieces such as "Tuna Fishing in Spain" and "Trout Fishing All Across Europe: Spain Has the Best, Then Germany"; and an article dedicated to bullfighting—"Pamplona in July; World's Series of Bull Fighting a Mad, Whirling Carnival". Hemingway was devastated on learning that Hadley had lost a suitcase filled with his manuscripts at the Gare de Lyon as she was traveling to Geneva to meet him in December 1922. The following September, because Hadley was pregnant, the couple returned to Toronto, where their son John Hadley Nicanor was born on October 10, 1923. During their absence Hemingway's first book, *Three Stories and Ten Poems*, was published. Two of the stories it contained were all that remained of his work after the loss of the suitcase, and the third had been written the previous spring in Italy. Within months a second volume, *in our time* (without capitals), was published. The small volume included six vignettes and a dozen stories Hemingway had written the previous summer during his first visit to Spain where he discovered the thrill of the *corrida*. He missed Paris, considered Toronto boring, and wanted to return to the life of a writer, rather than live the life of a journalist.

Hemingway, Hadley and their son (nicknamed Bumby), returned to Paris in January 1924 and moved into a new apartment on the Rue Notre Dame des Champs. Hemingway helped Ford Madox Ford edit the *transatlantic review* in which were published works by Pound, John Dos Passos, and Gertrude Stein as well as some of Hemingway's own early stories such as "Indian Camp". When *In Our Time* (with capital letters) was published in 1925, the dust jacket had comments from Ford. "Indian Camp" received considerable praise; Ford saw it as an important early story by a young writer, and critics in the United States claimed Hemingway reinvigorated the short story with his use of declarative sentences and his crisp style. Six months earlier, Hemingway met F. Scott Fitzgerald, and the pair formed a friendship of "admiration and hostility". Fitzgerald's *The Great Gatsby* had been published that year; Hemingway read it, liked it, and decided his next work had to be a novel.

Ernest, Hadley, and Bumby Hemingway in Schruns, Austria, in 1926, months before they separated

Since his first visit to see the bullfighting at the Festival of San Fermín in Pamplona in 1923, Hemingway was fascinated by the sport; he saw in it the brutality of war juxtaposed against a cruel beauty. In June 1925, Hemingway and Hadley left Paris for their annual visit to Pamplona accompanied by a group of American and British expatriates. The trip inspired Hemingway's first novel, *The Sun Also Rises*, which he began to write immediately after the fiesta, finishing in September. The novel presents the culture of bullfighting with the concept of *afición*, depicted as an authentic way of life, contrasted with the Parisian bohemians, depicted as inauthentic. Hemingway decided to slow his pace and devoted six months to the novel's rewrite. The manuscript arrived in New York in April, and he corrected the final proof in Paris in August 1926. Scribner's published the novel in October. *The Sun Also Rises* epitomized the post-war expatriate generation, received good reviews and is "recognized as Hemingway's greatest work". However, Hemingway himself later wrote to his editor Max Perkins that the "point of the book" was not so much about a generation being lost, but that "the earth abideth forever"; he believed the characters in *The Sun Also Rises* may have been "battered" but were not lost.

Hemingway's marriage to Hadley deteriorated as he was working on *The Sun Also Rises*. In the spring of 1926, Hadley became aware of his affair with Pauline Pfeiffer, although she endured Pauline's presence in Pamplona that July. On their return to Paris, Hadley and Hemingway decided to separate; and in November she formally requested a divorce. They split their possessions while Hadley accepted Hemingway's offer of the proceeds from *The Sun Also Rises*. The couple were divorced in January 1927, and Hemingway married Pauline Pfeiffer in May.

Pfeiffer was from Arkansas—her family was wealthy and Catholic—and before the marriage Hemingway converted to Catholicism. In Paris she worked for *Vogue*. After a honeymoon in Le Grau-du-Roi, where he contracted anthrax, Hemingway planned his next collection of short stories, *Men Without Women*, published in October 1927. By the end of the year Pauline, who was pregnant, wanted to move back to America. John Dos Passos recommended Key West, and they left Paris in March 1928. Some time that spring Hemingway suffered a severe injury in their Paris bathroom, when he pulled a skylight down on his head thinking he was pulling on a toilet chain. This left him with a prominent forehead scar, subject of numerous legends, which he carried for the rest of his life. When Hemingway was asked about the scar he was reluctant to answer. After his departure from Paris, Hemingway "never again lived in a big city".

### Key West and the Caribbean

Hemingway house in Key West, Florida where he lived with Pauline. He wrote *To Have and Have Not* in the second story pool house not seen in picture.

In the late spring Hemingway and Pauline traveled to Kansas City where their son Patrick Hemingway was born on June 28, 1928. Pauline had a difficult delivery, which Hemingway fictionalized in *A Farewell to Arms*. After Patrick's birth, Pauline and Hemingway traveled to Wyoming, Massachusetts and New York. In the fall he was in New York with Bumby, about to board a train to Florida, when he received a cable telling him that his father had committed suicide. Hemingway was devastated, having earlier sent a letter to his father telling him not to worry about financial difficulties; the letter arrived minutes after the suicide. He realized how Hadley must have felt after her own father's suicide in 1903, and he suggested, "I'll probably go the same way."

Upon his return to Key West in December, Hemingway worked on the draft of *A Farewell to Arms* before leaving for France in January. The draft had been finished in August but he delayed the revision. The serialization in *Scribner's Magazine* was scheduled to begin in May, but by April, Hemingway was still working on the ending, which he may have rewritten as many as seventeen times. *A Farewell to Arms* was published on September 27. Biographer James Mellow believes Hemingway's stature as an American writer was secured with the publication of *A Farewell to Arms*, which has a complexity not apparent in *The Sun Also Rises*. While in Spain during the summer of 1929, Hemingway researched his next work, *Death in the Afternoon*. He wanted to write a comprehensive treatise of bullfighting, with explanations of the *toreros* and *corridas*, complete with glossaries and appendices, because he believed bullfighting was "of great tragic interest, being literally of life and death."

During the early 1930s Hemingway spent his winters in Key West and summers in Wyoming, where he found "the most beautiful country he had seen in the American West" and hunting that included deer, elk, and grizzly bear. His third son, Gregory Hancock Hemingway, was born on November 12, 1931 in Kansas City. Pauline's uncle bought the couple a house in Key West with the second floor of the carriage house converted to a writing den. While in Key West he enticed his friends to join him on fishing expeditions—inviting Waldo Peirce, John Dos Passos, and Max Perkins—with one all male trip to the Dry Tortugas, and he frequented the local bar, Sloppy Joe's. He continued to travel to Europe and to Cuba, and although he wrote of Key West in 1933, "We have a fine house here, and kids are all well," Mellow believes he "was plainly restless."

Ernest, Pauline, Bumby, Patrick, and Gregory Hemingway pose with marlins after a fishing trip to Bimini in 1935

In 1933 Hemingway and Pauline went on safari to East Africa. The 10-week trip provided material for *Green Hills of Africa*, as well as the short stories "The Snows of Kilimanjaro" and "The Short Happy Life of Francis Macomber". They visited

Mombasa, Nairobi, and Machakos in Kenya, then on to Tanganyika, where they hunted in the Serengeti, around Lake Manyara and west and southeast of the present-day Tarangire National Park. Hemingway contracted amoebic dysentery that caused a prolapsed intestine, and he was evacuated by plane to Nairobi, an experience reflected in "The Snows of Kilimanjaro". Their guide was the noted "white hunter" Philip Hope Percival, who had guided Theodore Roosevelt on his 1909 safari. On his return to Key West in early 1934 Hemingway began work on *Green Hills of Africa*, published in 1935 to mixed reviews.

Hemingway bought a boat in 1934, named it the *Pilar*, and began sailing the Caribbean. In 1935 he first arrived at Bimini, where he spent a considerable amount of time. During this period he also worked on *To Have and Have Not*, published in 1937 while he was in Spain, the only novel he wrote during the 1930s.

Hemingway (center) with Dutch filmmaker Joris Ivens, and German writer Ludwig Renn (serving as an International Brigades officer) in Spain during Spanish Civil War, 1937.

**Spanish Civil War and World War II**

It was in Christmas 1936 when Hemingway first met war correspondent Martha Gellhorn at a bar in Key West, Florida. In 1937 Hemingway agreed to report on the Spanish Civil War for the North American Newspaper Alliance (NANA). In March he arrived in Spain with Dutch filmmaker Joris Ivens. Ivens, who was filming *The Spanish Earth*, needed Hemingway as a screenwriter to replace John Dos Passos, who left the project when his friend José Robles was arrested and later executed. The incident changed Dos Passos' opinion of the leftist republicans, which created a rift between him and Hemingway, who spread a rumor that Dos Passos was a coward for leaving Spain.

Martha Gellhorn went on to join him in Spain. Like Hadley, Martha was a native of St. Louis, and like Pauline, she had worked for *Vogue* in Paris. Of Martha, Kert explains, "she never catered to him the way other women did." Late in 1937, while in Madrid with Martha, Hemingway wrote his only play, *The Fifth Column*, as the city was being bombarded. He returned to Key West for a few months, then back to Spain twice in 1938. He was present at the Battle of the Ebro, the last republican stand, and was among fellow British and American journalists who were some of the last to leave the battle as they crossed the river.

Hemingway and sons Patrick (left) and Gregory, with three cats at *Finca Vigía* ca. 1942–1943. The Hemingways kept cats in Cuba 1942–1960. The polydactyl cats at Hemingway's Key West house arrived after the family's departure in 1940

In the spring of 1939, Hemingway crossed to Cuba in his boat to live in the Hotel Ambos Mundos in Havana. This was the separation phase of a slow and painful split from Pauline, which had begun when Hemingway met Martha. Martha soon joined him in Cuba, and they almost immediately rented "Finca Vigía" ("Lookout Farm"), a 15-acre (61,000 m) property 15 miles (24 km) from Havana. Pauline and the children left Hemingway that summer, after the family was re-united during a visit to Wyoming. After Hemingway's divorce from Pauline was finalized, he and Martha were married November 20, 1940, in Cheyenne, Wyoming. As he had after his divorce from Hadley, he changed locations; moving his primary summer residence to Ketchum, Idaho, just outside the newly built resort of Sun Valley, and his winter residence to Cuba. Hemingway, who had been disgusted when a Parisian friend allowed his cats to eat from the table, "developed a passion for cats" in Cuba, keeping dozens of them on the property.

Gellhorn inspired him to write his most famous novel, *For Whom the Bell Tolls*, which he started in March 1939, finished in July 1940, and was published in October 1940. Consistent with his pattern of moving around while working on a manuscript, he wrote *For Whom the Bell Tolls* in Cuba, Wyoming, and Sun Valley. *For Whom the Bell Tolls* became a book-of-the-month choice, sold half a million copies within months, was nominated for a Pulitzer Prize, and as Meyers describes, "triumphantly re-established Hemingway's literary reputation".

In January 1941 Martha was sent to China on assignment for *Collier's* magazine, and Hemingway accompanied her. Although Hemingway wrote dispatches for *PM*, he had little affinity for China. They had returned to Cuba before the declaration of war by the United States that December, and he convinced the Cuban government to help him refit the Pilar to ambush German submarines.

Hemingway with Col. Charles (Buck) T. Lanham in Germany, 1944, during the fighting in Hürtgenwald, after which he became ill with pneumonia.

During World War II, he was in Europe from June to December 1944. At the D-Day landing, military officials who considered him "precious cargo", kept him to a landing craft, although biographer Kenneth Lynn claims Hemingway fabricated accounts that he went ashore during the landings. Late in July he attached himself to "the 22nd Infantry Regiment commanded by Col. Charles 'Buck' Lanham, as it drove toward Paris", and he led a small band of village militia in Rambouillet, outside of Paris. Of Hemingway's exploits, World War II historian Paul Fussell remarks: "Hemingway got into considerable trouble playing infantry captain to a group of Resistance people that he gathered because a correspondent is not supposed to lead troops, even if he does it well". This was in fact in contraversion to the Geneva Convention, and Hemingway was brought up on formal charges; he said he "beat the rap" by claiming that his entire participation was to give advice. On August 25 he was present at the liberation of Paris, although the assertion that he was first in the city, or that he liberated the Ritz is considered part of the Hemingway legend. While in Paris he attended a reunion hosted by Sylvia Beach, and "made peace with" Gertrude Stein. Hemingway was present at heavy fighting in the Hürtgenwald near the end of 1944. On December 17, a feverish and ill Hemingway had himself driven to Luxembourg to cover what would later be called The Battle of the Bulge. However, as soon as he arrived, Lanham handed him to the doctors, who hospitalized him with pneumonia, and by the time he recovered a week later, the main fighting was over.

In 1947 Hemingway was awarded a Bronze Star for his bravery during World War II. He was recognized for his valor in having been "under fire in combat areas in order to obtain an accurate picture of conditions", with the commendation that "through his talent of expression, Mr. Hemingway enabled readers to obtain a vivid picture of the difficulties and triumphs of the front-line soldier and his organization in combat".

When Hemingway initially arrived in England, he met *Time* magazine correspondent Mary Welsh in London, and was infatuated. Martha—who had been forced to cross the Atlantic in a ship filled with explosives because he refused to help her get a press pass on a plane—arrived in London to find Hemingway hospitalized with a concussion from a car accident. Unsympathetic to his plight, she accused him of being a bully, and told him she was "through, absolutely finished." The last time he saw her was in March 1945, as he was preparing to return to Cuba. Meanwhile, he had asked Mary Welsh to marry him on their third meeting.

### Cuba and the Nobel Prize

Hemingway said he "was out of business as a writer" from 1942 to 1945. In 1946 he married Mary, who had an ectopic pregnancy five months later. Hemingway and Mary had a series of accidents and health problems after the war: in a 1945 car accident he "smashed his knee" and sustained another "deep wound on his forehead"; Mary broke her right ankle and then her left ankle in successive skiing accidents. In 1947 his sons Patrick and Gregory were in a car accident, leaving Patrick with a head wound and severely ill. Hemingway became depressed as his literary friends died: in 1939 Yeats and Ford Madox Ford; in 1940 Scott Fitzgerald; in 1941 Sherwood Anderson and James Joyce; in 1946 Gertrude Stein; and the following year in 1947, Max Perkins, Hemingway's long time Scribner's editor and friend. During this period he had severe headaches, high blood pressure, weight problems, and eventually diabetes—much of which was the result of previous accidents and heavy drinking. Nonetheless, early in 1946 he began work on *The Garden of Eden*, finishing 800 pages by June. During the post–war years he also began work on a trilogy to be called "The Land", "The Sea" and "The Air" which he intended to combine in one novel titled *The Sea Book*. However, both projects stalled and Mellow considers Hemingway's inability to continue "a symptom of his troubles" during these years.

In 1948 Hemingway and Mary traveled to Europe. During a several months long stay in Venice he fell in love with the then 19 year old Adriana Ivancich. The platonic love affair inspired the novel *Across the River and Into the Trees*, published in 1950 to bad reviews. The relationship with Adriana lasted until 1955.. In 1951 Hemingway wrote the draft of *Old Man and the Sea* in eight weeks, considering it "the best I can write ever for all of my life". *The Old Man and the Sea* became a book-of-the-month selection, made Hemingway an international celebrity, and won the Pulitzer Prize in May 1952, a month before he left for his second trip to Africa.

Hemingway at a fishing camp. His hand and arms are burned from a recent brushfire; his hair burned from the recent plane crashes.

In Africa he was seriously injured in two successive plane crashes. Hemingway chartered a sightseeing flight of the Belgian Congo as a Christmas present to Mary. On their way to photograph Murchison Falls from the air, the plane struck an abandoned utility pole and "crash landed in heavy brush." Hemingway's injuries included a head wound, while Mary broke two ribs. The next day, attempting to reach medical care in Entebbe, they boarded a second plane that exploded at take-off with Hemingway suffering burns and another concussion, this one serious enough to cause leaking of cerebral fluid. They eventually arrived in Entebbe to find reporters covering the story of Hemingway's death. He briefed the reporters, and spent the next few weeks recuperating and reading his obituaries. Despite his injuries, Hemingway accompanied Patrick and his wife on a planned fishing expedition in February, but pain caused him to be irascible and difficult to get along with. When a bushfire broke out he was again injured, with second degree burns on his legs, front torso, lips, left hand and right forearm. Months later in Venice, "according to Mary they learned the full extent of Hemingway's injuries". She reported to friends that he had two cracked discs, a kidney and liver rupture, a dislocated shoulder and a broken skull. The accidents may have precipitated the physical deterioration that was to follow.

After the plane crashes, Hemingway, who had been "a thinly controlled alcoholic throughout much of his life, drank more heavily than usual to combat the pain of his injuries."

Ernest Hemingway in the cabin of his boat Pilar, off the coast of Cuba

In October 1954 Hemingway received the Nobel Prize in Literature. He modestly told the press that Carl Sandburg, Isak Dinesen and Bernard Berenson deserved the prize, but the prize money would be welcome. Mellow claims Hemingway "had coveted the Nobel Prize", but when he won it, months after his plane accidents and the ensuing world-wide press coverage, "there must have been a lingering suspicion in Hemingway's mind that his obituary notices had played a part in the academy's decision." Because he was suffering pain from the African accidents, he decided against traveling to Stockholm. Instead he sent a speech to be read, defining the writer's life: "Writing, at its best, is a lonely life. Organizations for writers palliate the writer's loneliness but I doubt if they improve his writing. He grows in public stature as he sheds his loneliness and often his work deteriorates. For he does his work alone and if he is a good enough writer he must face eternity, or the lack of it, each day."

From the end of the year in 1955 to early 1956, Hemingway was bedridden. He was told to stop drinking to mitigate liver damage, advice he initially followed but then disregarded. In October 1956 he returned to Europe and met Basque writer Pio Baroja, who was seriously ill and died weeks later. During the trip Hemingway became sick again, and was treated for "high blood pressure, liver disease, and arteriosclerosis".

In November, while in Paris, he was reminded of trunks he had stored in the Ritz Hotel in 1928 and never retrieved. The trunks were filled with notebooks and writing from his Paris years. Excited about the discovery, when he returned to Cuba in 1957 he began to shape the recovered work into his memoir *A Moveable Feast*. By 1959 he ended a period of intense activity: he finished *A Moveable Feast* (scheduled to be released the following year); brought *True at First Light* to 200,000 words; added chapters to *The Garden of Eden*; and worked on *Islands in the Stream*. The latter three were stored in a safe deposit box in Havana, as he focused on the finishing touches for *A Moveable Feast*. Reynolds claims that it was during this period he slid into depression, from which he was unable to recover.

The Finca Vigia became crowded with guests and tourists, as Hemingway, beginning to become unhappy with life there, considered a permanent move to Idaho. In 1959 he bought a home overlooking the Big Wood River, outside of Ketchum, and left Cuba—although he apparently remained on easy terms with the Castro government, telling the *New York Times* he was "delighted" with Castro's overthrow of Havana. He was in Cuba in November 1959, between returning from Pamplona and traveling west to Idaho, and the following year for his birthday; however, that year he and Mary decided to leave after hearing the news that Castro wanted to nationalize property owned by Americans and other foreign nationals. In July 1960 the Hemingways left Cuba for the last time, leaving art and manuscripts in a bank vault in Havana. After the 1961 Bay of Pigs Invasion, the Finca Vigia was expropriated by the Cuban government, complete with Hemingway's collection of "four to six thousand books".

## Idaho and suicide

Hemingway bird-hunting at Silver Creek, near Picabo, Idaho, January 1959. With him is Gary Cooper and local resident Bobbie Peterson.

He continued to work on *A Moveable Feast* through the end of the 1950s, and in the summer of 1959 he visited Spain to research a series of bullfighting articles for *Life Magazine*. Back in Ketchum at Christmas he appeared to be suffering from paranoia; at a restaurant one night with friends, he claimed the lights were on in the adjacent bank building because the FBI were "checking our accounts". By January he returned to Cuba and continued work on the *Life* magazine series. The manuscript grew to 63,000 words—*Life* wanted only 10,000 words—and he asked A. E. Hotchner to help organize the work that would become *The Dangerous Summer*. Hotchner found Hemingway to be "unusually hesitant, disorganized, and confused".

Although Hemingway's mental deterioration was noticeable in the summer of 1960, he again traveled to Spain to obtain photographs for the manuscript. Without Mary, he was lonely and took to his bed for days, retreating into silence. The first installments of *The Dangerous Summer* were published in *Life* in September 1960 to good reviews. When he left Spain, he went straight to Idaho, but was worried about money and his safety. As his paranoia increased, he believed the FBI was actively monitoring his movements. Hemingway suffered from physical problems as well: his health declined and his eyesight was failing. In November he was admitted to the Mayo Clinic in Minnesota, where he may have believed he was to be treated for hypertension. Meyers writes that "an aura of secrecy surrounds Hemingway's treatment at the Mayo", but confirms that in December 1960 he received electroconvulsive therapy as many as 15 times, then in January 1961 he was "released in ruins".

Ernest and Mary Hemingway are buried in the town cemetery in Ketchum, Idaho.

Three months later, back in Ketchum, Mary found Hemingway holding a shotgun one morning. She called Dr. Saviers, who sedated him and had him admitted to the Sun Valley Hospital; from there he was returned to the Mayo for more shock treatments. He was released in late June and arrived home in Ketchum on June 30. Two days later, in the early morning hours of July 2, 1961, Hemingway "quite deliberately" shot himself with his favorite shotgun. He unlocked the gun cabinet, went to the front entrance of their Ketchum home, and "pushed two shells into the twelve-gauge Boss shotgun, put the end of the barrel into his mouth, pulled the trigger and blew out his brains." Mary called the Sun Valley Hospital, and Dr. Scott Earle arrived at the house within "fifteen minutes". Despite his finding that Hemingway "had died of a self-inflicted wound to the head", the story told to the press was that the death had been "accidental".

During his final years, Hemingway's behavior was similar to his father's before he himself committed suicide; his father may have had the genetic disease hemochromatosis, in which the inability to metabolize iron culminates in mental and physical deterioration. Medical records made available in 1991 confirm that Hemingway's hemochromatosis had been diagnosed in early 1961. His sister Ursula and his brother Leicester also committed suicide. Added to Hemingway's physical ailments was the additional problem that he had been a heavy drinker for most of his life. Writing in "Ernest Hemingway: A Psychological Autopsy of a Suicide", Christopher Martin evaluates the causes of the suicide: "Careful reading of Hemingway's major biographies and his personal and public writings reveals evidence suggesting the presence of the following conditions during his lifetime: bipolar disorder, alcohol dependence, traumatic brain injury, and probable borderline and narcissistic personality traits". Martin claims suicide was inevitable because Hemingway "suffered from an enormous burden of psychiatric comorbidities and risk factors for suicide", although without a clinical evaluation of the patient, Martin concedes a diagnosis is difficult.

Hemingway's family and friends flew to Ketchum for the funeral, which was officiated by the local Catholic priest, who believed the death accidental. Of the funeral (during which an altar boy fainted at the head of the casket), his brother Leicester wrote: "It seemed to me Ernest would have approved of it all."

In a press interview five years later Mary Hemingway admitted her husband had committed suicide.

## Writing style

The *New York Times* wrote in 1926 of Hemingway's first novel: "No amount of analysis can convey the quality of *The Sun Also Rises*. It is a truly gripping story, told in a lean, hard, athletic narrative prose that puts more literary English to shame." *The Sun Also Rises* is written in the spare, tightly written prose, for which Hemingway is famous; a style that has influenced countless crime and pulp fiction novels. In 1954, when Hemingway was awarded the Nobel Prize for Literature, it was for "his mastery of the art of narrative, most recently demonstrated in *The Old Man and the Sea*, and for the influence that he has exerted on contemporary style."

Henry Louis Gates believes Hemingway's style was fundamentally shaped "in reaction to [his] experience of world war". After World War I, he and other modernists "lost faith in the central institutions of Western civilization," by reacting against the "elaborate style" of 19th century writers; and by creating a style "in which meaning is established through dialogue, through action, and silences—a fiction in which nothing crucial—or at least very little—is stated explicitly."

Because he began as a writer of short stories, Baker believes Hemingway learned to "get the most from the least, how to prune language, how to multiply intensities and how to tell nothing but the truth in a way that allowed for telling more than the truth." Hemingway referred to his style as the iceberg theory: in his writing the facts float above water; the supporting structure and symbolism operate out-of-sight. Writing in "The Art of the Short Story," he explains: "A few things I have found to be true. If you leave out important things or events that you know about, the story is strengthened. If you leave or skip something because you do not know it, the story will be worthless. The test of any story is how very good the stuff that you, not your editors, omit."

Jackson Benson believes Hemingway used autobiographical details as framing devices about life in general—not only about his life. For example, Benson postulates that Hemingway used his experiences and drew them out with "what if" scenarios: "what if I were wounded in such a way that I could not sleep at night? What if I were wounded and made crazy, what would happen if I were sent back to the front?" The concept of the iceberg theory is sometimes referred to as the "theory of omission." Hemingway believed the writer could describe one thing (such as Nick Adams fishing in "The Big Two-Hearted River") though an entirely different thing occurs below the surface (Nick Adams concentrating on fishing to the extent that he does not have to think about anything else).

The simplicity of the prose is deceptive. Zoe Trodd believes Hemingway crafted skeletal sentences in response to Henry James's observation that World War I had "used up words." Hemingway offers a "multi-focal" photographic reality. His iceberg theory of omission is the foundation on which he builds. The syntax, which lacks subordinating conjunctions, creates static sentences. The photographic "snapshot" style creates a collage of images. Many types of internal punctuation (colons, semicolons, dashes, parentheses) are omitted in favor of short declarative sentences. The sentences build on each other, as events build to create a sense of the whole. Multiple strands exist in one story; an "embedded text" bridges to a different angle. He also uses other cinematic techniques of "cutting" quickly from one scene to the next; or of "splicing" a scene into another. Intentional omissions allow the reader to fill the gap, as though responding to instructions from the author, and create three-dimensional prose.

In his literature, and in his personal writing, Hemingway habitually used the word "and" in place of commas. This use of polysyndeton may serve to convey immediacy. Hemingway's polysyndetonic sentence—or in later works his use of subordinate clauses—uses conjunctions to juxtapose startling visions and images; Jackson Benson compares them to haikus. Many of Hemingway's followers misinterpreted his lead and frowned upon all expression of emotion; Saul Bellow satirized this style as "Do you have emotions? Strangle them." However, Hemingway's intent was not to eliminate emotion, but to portray it more scientifically. Hemingway thought it would be easy, and pointless, to describe emotions; he sculpted collages of images in order to grasp "the real thing, the sequence of motion and fact which made the emotion and which would be as valid in a year or in ten years or, with luck and if you stated it purely enough, always." This use of an image as an objective correlative is characteristic of Ezra Pound, T. S. Eliot, James Joyce, and Proust. Hemingway's letters refer to Proust's *Remembrance of Things Past* several times over the years, and indicate he read the book at least twice. His writing was likely also influenced by the Japanese poetic canon.

## Themes

Recurring themes in American literature exist with clarity in Hemingway's work. Leslie Fiedler sees the theme he defines as "The Sacred Land"—the American West—extended in Hemingway's work, to include mountains in Spain, Switzerland and Africa, and to the streams of Michigan. The American West is given a symbolic nod with the naming of the "Hotel Montana" in *The Sun Also Rises* and *For Whom the Bell Tolls*. Although Hemingway writes about sports, Carlos Baker believes the emphasis is more on the athlete than the sport. According to Stoltzfus and Fiedler, Hemingway's nature is a place for rebirth, for therapy, and the hunter or fisherman has a moment of transcendence when the prey is killed. Nature is where men are without women: men fish; men hunt; men find redemption in nature.

Fiedler believes Hemingway inverts the American literary theme of the evil "Dark Woman" versus the good "Light Woman". The dark woman—Brett Ashley of *The Sun Also Rises*—is a goddess; the light woman—Margot Macomber of "The Short Happy Life of Francis Macomber"—is a murderess. Robert Sholes admits that early Hemingway stories, such as "A Very Short Story", present "a male character favorably and a female unfavorably." According to Rena Sanderson, early Hemingway critics lauded his male-centric world of masculine pursuits, and the fiction divided women into "castrators or love-slaves." Feminist critics attacked Hemingway as "public enemy number one", although more recent re-evaluations of his work "have given new visibility to Hemingway's female characters (and their strengths) and have revealed his own sensitivity to gender issues, thus casting doubts on the old assumption that his writings were one-sidedly masculine." Nina Baym believes that Brett Ashley and Margot Macomber "are the two outstanding examples of Hemingway's 'bitch women.'"

The theme of women and death is evident in stories as early as "Indian Camp". The theme of death permeates Hemingway's work. Young believes the emphasis in "Indian Camp" was not so much on the woman who gives birth or the father who commits suicide, but on Nick Adams who witnesses these events as a child, and becomes a "badly scarred and nervous young man." Hemingway sets the events in "Indian Camp" that shape the Adams persona. Young believes "Indian Camp" holds the "master key" to "what its author was up to for some thirty-five years of his writing career." Stoltzfus considers Hemingway's work to be more complex with a representation of the truth inherent in existentialism: if "nothingness" is embraced, then redemption is achieved at the moment of death. Those who face death with dignity and courage live an authentic life. Francis Macomber dies happy because the last hours of his life are authentic; the bullfighter in the corrida represents the pinnacle of a life lived with authenticity. In his paper *The Uses of Authenticity: Hemingway and the Literary Field*, Timo Müller writes that Hemingway's fiction is successful because the characters live an "authentic life", and the "soldiers, fishers, boxers and backwoodsmen are among the archetypes of authenticity in modern literature".

The theme of emasculation is prevalent in Hemingway's work, most notably in *The Sun Also Rises*. Emasculation, according to Fiedler, is a result of a generation of wounded soldiers; and of a generation in which women such as Brett gained emancipation. This also applies to the minor character, Frances Clyne, Cohn's girlfriend in the beginning in the book. Her character supports the theme not only because the idea was presented early on in the novel but also the impact she had on Cohn in the start of the book while only appearing a small number of times. Baker believes Hemingway's work emphasizes the "natural" versus the "unnatural". In "Alpine Idyll" the "unnaturalness" of skiing in the high country late spring snow is juxtaposed against the "unnaturalness" of the peasant who allowed his wife's dead body to linger too long in the shed during the winter. The skiers and peasant retreat to the valley to the "natural" spring for redemption.

Some critics have characterized Hemingway's work as misogynistic and homophobic. Susan Beegel analyzed four decades of Hemingway criticism, published in her essay "Critical Reception". She found, particularly in the 1980s, "critics interested in multiculturalism" simply ignored Hemingway; although some "apologetics" have been written. Typical is this analysis of *The Sun Also Rises*: "Hemingway never lets the reader forget that Cohn is a Jew, not an unattractive character who happens to be a Jew but a character who is unattractive because he is a Jew." During the same decade, according to Beegel, criticism was published that investigated the "horror of homosexuality", and racism in Hemingway's fiction.

## Influence and legacy

Statue of Hemingway by José Villa Soberón, *El Floridita* bar in Havana, with a photo of Hemingway awarding Fidel Castro a prize in a fishing contest in 1960 (after the Cuban revolution) on the wall.

Hemingway's legacy to American literature is his style: writers who came after him emulated it or avoided it. After his reputation was sealed with the publication of *The Sun Also Rises*, he became the spokesperson for the post–World War I generation, having established a style to follow. His books were burned in Berlin in 1933, "as being a monument of modern decadence", and disavowed by his parents as "filth". Reynolds asserts the legacy is that "he left stories and novels so starkly moving that some have become part of our cultural heritage." In a 2004 speech at the John F. Kennedy Library, Russell Banks declared that he, like many male writers of his generation, was influenced by Hemingway's writing philosophy, style, and public image. Conversely, as early as the 1930s Hemingway's style was parodied, and criticized as "lazy" within the context of the "American literary tradition."

Benson believes the details of Hemingway's life have become a "prime vehicle for exploitation", resulting in a Hemingway industry. Hemingway scholar Hallengren believes the "hard boiled style" and the machismo must be separated from the author himself. Benson agrees, describing him as introverted and private as J. D. Salinger, although Hemingway masked his nature with braggadocio. In fact, during World War II, Salinger met and corresponded with Hemingway, whom he acknowledged as an influence. In a letter to Hemingway, Salinger claimed their talks "had given him his only hopeful minutes of the entire war" and jokingly "named himself national chairman of the Hemingway Fan Clubs."

The extent of Hemingway's influence is seen in the tributes and echoes of his fiction in popular culture. A minor planet, discovered in 1978 by Soviet astronomer Nikolai Stepanovich Chernykh, was named for him (3656 Hemingway); Ray Bradbury wrote *The Kilimanjaro Device*, with Hemingway transported to the top of Mount Kilimanjaro; the 1993 motion picture *Wrestling Ernest Hemingway*, about the friendship of two retired men, Irish and Cuban, in a seaside town in Florida, starred Robert Duvall, Richard Harris, Shirley MacLaine, Sandra Bullock, and Piper Laurie. The influence is evident with the many restaurants named "Hemingway"; and the proliferation of bars called "Harry's" (a nod to the bar in

Across the River and Into the Trees). A line of Hemingway furniture, promoted by Hemingway's son Jack (Bumby), has pieces such as the "Kilimanjaro" bedside table, and a "Catherine" slip-covered sofa. Montblanc offers a Hemingway fountain pen, and a line of Hemingway safari clothes has been created. The International Imitation Hemingway Competition was created in 1977 to publicly acknowledge his influence and the comically misplaced efforts of lesser authors to imitate his style. Entrants are encouraged to submit one "really good page of really bad Hemingway" and winners are flown to Italy to Harry's Bar.

In 1965 Mary Hemingway established the Hemingway Foundation and in the 1970s she donated her husband's papers to the John F. Kennedy Library. In 1980 a group of Hemingway scholars gathered to assess the donated papers, subsequently forming the Hemingway Society, "committed to supporting and fostering Hemingway scholarship."

Almost exactly 35 years after Hemingway's death, on July 1, 1996, his granddaughter Margaux Hemingway died in Santa Monica, California. Margaux was a supermodel and actress, co-starring with her sister Mariel in the 1976 movie *Lipstick*. Her death was later ruled a suicide, making her "the fifth person in four generations of her family to commit suicide." Margaux's sister, Mariel, is an actress, model, writer and film producer.

### Selected list of works
- "Indian Camp" (1926)
- *The Sun Also Rises* (1926)
- *A Farewell to Arms* (1929)
- "The Short Happy Life of Francis Macomber" (1935)
- *For Whom the Bell Tolls* (1940)
- *The Old Man and the Sea* (1951)
- *A Moveable Feast* (1964, posthumous)
- *True at First Light* (1999)

Source (edited): "http://en.wikipedia.org/wiki/Ernest_Hemingway"

## Ernest Hemingway: The Collected Stories

***Ernest Hemingway: The Collected Stories*** is a posthumous collection of Hemingway's short fiction, published in 1995. Introduced by James Fenton it is considered to be the most complete compendium of Hemingway's short stories. It is published in the UK only by Random House as part of the Everyman Library. The collection is split in two parts.

Part One contains the four individual collections of stories Hemingway published during his lifetime. They are the tiny experimental prose volume, *in our time* (1924), the much expanded *In Our Time* (1925, with an extra story added in 1930), *Men Without Women* (1927) and *Winner Take Nothing* (1933). In addition, four further stories were first published in Hemingway's first omnibus, *The Fifth Column and the First Forty-Nine Stories* (1938).

Part Two contains anomalous stories which were added to the collections Hemingway (and others) have since published. It is also includes some stories, fragments and juvenilia that have never before been published in book-form. The collection does, however, limit itself to material that had already appeared in print.

Some material, first published in *The Complete Short Stories* (1987), is not included in this edition, as Fenton determined that it was not properly classified as short stories. This includes "One Trip Across" and "Tradesman's Return" (the first two parts of *To Have and Have Not*); and "An African Story" (fillited from various chapters of *The Garden of Eden*—itself a posthumous novel).

### Part One: Stories Collected in Hemingway's Lifetime
- **From *Three Stories and Ten Poems* (1923)**
  - Up in Michigan (1923, revised 1938)
- ***in our time* (1924)**
- ***In Our Time* (1925 and 1930)**
  - On the Quai at Smyrna
  - Indian Camp
  - The Doctor and the Doctor's Wife
  - The End of Something
  - The Three-Day Blow
  - The Battler
  - A Very Short Story
  - Soldier's Home
  - The Revolutionist
  - Mr. And Mrs. Elliot
  - Cat in the Rain
  - Out of Season
  - Cross-Country Snow
  - My Old Man
  - Big Two-Hearted River, Part I
  - Big Two-Hearted River, Part II
- ***Men Without Women* (1927)**
  - The Undefeated
  - In Another Country
  - Hills Like White Elephants
  - The Killers
  - Che Ti Dice La Patria?
  - Fifty Grand
  - A Simple Enquiry
  - Ten Indians
  - A Canary for One
  - An Alpine Idyll
  - A Pursuit Race
  - Today is Friday
  - Banal Story
  - Now I Lay Me
- ***Winner Take Nothing* (1933)**
  - After the Storm
  - A Clean, Well-Lighted Place
  - The Light of the World
  - God Rest You Merry, Gentlemen
  - The Sea Change
  - A Way You'll Never Be
  - The Mother of a Queen
  - One Reader Writes
  - Homage to Switzerland
  - A Day's Wait
  - A Natural History of the Dead
  - Wine of Wyoming
  - The Gambler, the Nun, and the Radio
  - Fathers and Sons
- **Stories from *The Fifth Column and the First Forty-Nine Stories* (1938)**
  - The Capital of the World

- The Snows of Kilimanjaro
- The Short Happy Life of Francis Macomber (1936)
- Old Man at the Bridge (1938)

**Part Two: Stories and Fragments from Posthumous Collections**
- **Uncollected Stories published in Hemingway's Lifetime**
  - The Denunciation (1938)
  - The Butterfly and the Tank (1938)
  - Night Before Battle (1939)
  - Under the Ridge (1939)
  - Nobody Ever Dies (1939)
  - The Good Lion (1951)
  - The Faithful Bull (1951)
  - A Man of the World (1957)
  - Get a Seeing-Eyed Dog (1957)
- **Drafts and Fragments first published in *The Nick Adams Stories* (1972)**
  - Three Shots
  - The Indians Moved Away
  - The Last Good Country
  - Crossing the Mississippi
  - Night Before Landing
  - Summer People
  - Wedding Day
  - On Writing
- **First published in *The Complete Short Stories* (1987)**
  - A Train Trip
  - The Porter
  - Black Ass at the Crossroads
  - Landscape with Figures
  - I Guess Everything Reminds You of Something
  - Great News from the Mainland
  - The Strange Country
- **Juvenilia and Pre-Paris Stories**
  - Judgment of Manitou (1916)
  - A Matter of Colour (1916)
  - Sepi Jingan (1916)
  - The Mercenaries (1985)
  - Crossroads – an Anthology (1985)
  - Portrait of the Idealist in Love (1985)
  - The Ash Heel's Tendon (1985)
  - The Current (1985)

Source (edited): "http://en.wikipedia.org/wiki/Ernest_Hemingway:_The_Collected_Stories"

# Ernest Hemingway Selected Letters 1917–1961

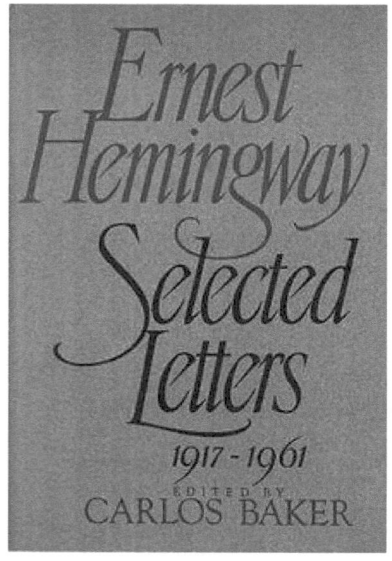

1st edition (publ. Scribner)

*Ernest Hemingway Selected Letters 1917–1961* is a book composed of letters to and from Ernest Hemingway found at his Cuban home after his death, edited by Hemingway biographer Carlos Baker.

Hemingway was a prolific correspondent and in 1981 many of his letters were published by Scribner's in the volume. Although Hemingway wrote to his executors in 1958 asking that his letters not be published, in 1979 his wife Mary Hemingway made the decision to have the letters published.

Source (edited): "http://en.wikipedia.org/wiki/Ernest_Hemingway_Selected_Letters_1917%E2%80%931961"

# Ernest Hemingway bibliography

This is a list of works by Ernest Hemingway (1899–1961). This list includes his novels, short stories and non-fiction as well as film and television adaptations of his works.

## Posthumous works

These literary works were published after Hemingway's death.
- (1964) *A Moveable Feast*
- (1969) *The Fifth Column and Four Stories of the Spanish Civil War*
- (1970) *Islands in the Stream*
- (1972) *The Nick Adams Stories*
- (1985) *The Dangerous Summer*
- (1986) *The Garden of Eden*
- (1987) *The Complete Short Stories Of Ernest Hemingway*
- (1999) *True at First Light*
- (2003) *Selected Letters 1917–1961*

Source (edited): "http://en.wikipedia.org/wiki/Ernest_Hemingway_bibliography"

# Fathers and Sons (short story)

"Fathers and Sons" is a short story by Ernest Hemingway, and is a part of *The Nick Adams Stories*. The story can be broken into two parts: the first, wherein Nick and his son are on their way to Nick's hometown, and the second, the time the two spend in the town.

## Synopsis

The story is about a father, Nick, and his son, who are returning to Nick's hometown. On the way, Nick is continuously questioned by his son about what the town is like, which makes Nick think of how his hometown used to be, what he used to do, and what his relationship was with his parents, in particularly with his father (whom he greatly admired). He begins to reflect on the times with his father, thinking about how he will choose to pass the memory of his father to his son.

Once they have arrived, Nick sees that nothing is like it used to be, as no one lives there anymore. He decided that he should make the memory of his father a better memory for his son. Based on experience, he realizes that he should be a better father than his own father.

Important themes in "Fathers and Sons" include the father/son relationship, Nick's homecoming, youth/childhood/adolescence, the contrasts of Trudy and Nick's father, melancholy, role models, roles changing, and identity forming.

Source (edited): "http://en.wikipedia.org/wiki/Fathers_and_Sons_(short_story)"

# *For Whom the Bell Tolls*

*For Whom the Bell Tolls* is a novel by Ernest Hemingway published in 1940. It tells the story of Robert Jordan, a young American in the International Brigades attached to a republican guerrilla unit during the Spanish Civil War. As an expert in the use of explosives, he is assigned to blow up a bridge during an attack on the city of Segovia. Hemingway biographer Jeffrey Meyers writes the novel is regarded as one of Hemingway's best works, along with *The Sun Also Rises*, *The Old Man and the Sea*, and *A Farewell to Arms*.

## Origin of book title

The title of the book quotes John Donne's Meditation no. 17 from "Devotions upon Emergent Occasions" (1624): "No man is an island, entire of itself; every man is a piece of the continent, a part of the main. If a clod be washed away by the sea, Europe is the less, as well as if a promontory were, as well as if a manor of thy friend's or of thine own were: any man's death diminishes me, because I am involved in mankind, and therefore never send to know *for whom the bell tolls*; it tolls for thee."

## Plot summary

This novel is told primarily through the thoughts and experiences of Robert Jordan, a character inspired by Hemingway's own experiences in the Spanish Civil War. Robert Jordan is an American who travels to Spain to oppose the nationalist forces of Francisco Franco.

A superior has ordered him to travel behind enemy lines and destroy a bridge, using the aid of a group of guerrillas who have been living in the mountains nearby. In their camp, Robert Jordan encounters María, a young Spanish native whose life has been shattered by the outbreak of the war. His strong sense of duty clashes with both Republican partisan leader Pablo's fear and unwillingness to commit to a covert operation that would have repercussions, and his own *joie de vivre* that is kindled by his newfound love for María.

The novel graphically describes the brutality of civil war.

## Characters

- Robert Jordan – American university instructor of Spanish language and a specialist in demolitions and explosives.
- Anselmo - Elderly guide to Robert Jordan.
- Golz - Commander who ordered the bridge's demolition.
- Pablo - Leader of a group of antifascist guerrillas.
- Rafael – Incompetent, lazy guerrilla, and a gypsy.
- María – Robert Jordan's young lover.
- Pilar – Wife of Pablo. An aged but strong woman, she is the de facto leader of the guerrilla band.
- Agustín – Foul-mouthed, middle-aged guerrilla.
- El Sordo – Leader of a fellow band of guerrillas.
- Fernando – Middle-aged guerrilla.
- Andrés and Eladio – Brothers. Members of Pablo's band.
- Primitivo – Young guerrilla in Pablo's band.
- Joaquin – Enthusiastic teenaged communist, member of Sordo's band.

## Background

Hemingway wrote *For Whom the Bell Tolls* in Cuba, Key West, and Sun Valley, Idaho in 1939. In Cuba, he lived in the Hotel Ambos-Mundos where he worked on the manuscript. The novel was finished in July 1940, and published in October. The novel is based on his experiences during the Spanish Civil War, with an American protagonist named Robert Jordan who fights with Spanish soldiers for the republicans. The novel has three types of characters: those who are purely fictional; those based on real people but fictionalized; and those who were actual figures in the war. Set in the Sierra de Guadarrama mountain range between Madrid and Segovia, the action takes place during four days and three nights. *For Whom the Bell Tolls* became a Book-of-the-month choice, sold half a million copies within months, was nominated for a Pulitzer Prize, and became a literary triumph for Hemingway. Published on 21 October 1940, the first edition print run was 75,000 copies priced at $2.75.

## Main themes

Death is a primary preoccupation of the novel. When Robert Jordan is assigned to blow up the bridge, he knows that he will not survive it. Pablo and El Sordo, leaders of the Republican guerrilla bands, see that inevitability also. Almost all of the main characters in the book contemplate their own deaths.

Hotel Ambos-Mundos (*Hotel of Both-Worlds*), Havana, Ernest Hemingway's first residence in Cuba (1932–1939) where the first chapter of *For Whom the Bell Tolls* was written. Much of the rest was written later in his home near Havana, Finca Vigía (Lookout Farm)

There is camaraderie in the face of death throughout the novel, with the need for surrender of one's self for the common good repeated. Robert Jordan, Anselmo and others are ready to do "as all good men should" – that is, to make the ultimate sacrifice. The oft-repeated embracing gesture reinforces this sense of close companionship in the face of death. An incident involving the death of the character Joaquín's family serves as an excellent example of this theme. Having learned of this tragedy, Joaquín's comrades embrace and comfort him, saying they now are his family. Surrounding this love for one's comrades is the love for the Spanish soil. A love of place, of the senses, and of life itself is represented by the pine needle forest floor – both at the beginning and, poignantly, at the end of the novel – when Robert Jordan awaits his death feeling "his heart beating against the pine needle floor of the forest."

Suicide always looms as an alternative to suffering. Many of the characters, including Robert Jordan, would prefer death over capture and are prepared to kill themselves, be killed, or kill to avoid it. As the book ends, Robert Jordan, wounded and unable to travel with his companions, awaits a final ambush that will end his life. He prepares himself against the cruel outcomes of suicide to avoid capture, or inevitable torture for the extraction of information and death at the hands of the enemy. Still, he hopes to avoid suicide partly because his father, whom he views as a coward, committed suicide. Robert Jordan understands suicide but doesn't approve of it, and thinks that "you have to be awfully occupied with yourself to do a thing like that." Robert Jordan's opinions on suicide may be used to analyze Hemingway's suicide 21 years later. Hemingway's father also committed suicide and it is a common theme in his works.

The novel explores political ideologies and the nature of bigotry. After noticing how he so easily employed the convenient catch-phrase "enemy of the people", Jordan moves swiftly into the subjects and opines, "To be bigoted you have to be absolutely sure that you are right and nothing makes that surety and righteousness like continence. Continence is the foe of heresy." Later in the book, Robert Jordan explains the threat of Fascism in his own country. "Robert Jordan, wiping out the stew bowl with bread, explained how the income tax and inheritance tax worked. 'But the big estates remain. Also, there are taxes on the land,' he said. 'But surely the big proprietors and the rich will make a revolution against such taxes. Such taxes appear to me to be revolutionary. They will revolt against the government when they see that they are threatened, exactly as the fascists have done here,' Primitivo said. 'It is possible.' 'Then you will have to fight in your country as we fight here.' 'Yes, we will have to fight.' 'But are there not many fascists in your country?' 'There are many who do not know they are fascists but will find it out when the time comes.'" Also in the same conversation Robert Jordan is having with the others, he realizes how there are populist policies right in America, namely homesteading which was widely used by American settlers to settle the West from 1863 onward : "Robert Jordan explained the process of homesteading. He had never thought of it before as an agrarian reform. 'That is magnificent,' Primitivo said. 'Then you have a communism in your country?' 'No. That is done under the Republic.'"

Divination emerges as an alternative means of perception. Pilar, "Pablo's woman", is a reader of palms and more. When Robert Jordan questions her true abilities, she replies, "Because thou art a miracle of deafness.... It is not that thou art stupid. Thou art simply deaf. One who is deaf cannot hear music. Neither can he hear the radio. So he might say, never having heard them, that such things do not exist."

## Imagery

Hemingway frequently used images to produce the dense atmosphere of violence and death his books are renowned for; the main image of *For Whom the Bell Tolls* is the machine image. As he had done in "A Farewell to Arms", Hemingway employs the fear of modern armament to destroy romantic conceptions of the ancient art of war: combat, sportsmanlike competition and the aspect of hunting. Heroism becomes butchery: the most powerful picture employed here is the shooting of María's parents against the wall of a slaughterhouse. Glory exists in the official dispatches only; here, the "disillusionment" theme of *A Farewell to Arms* is adapted.

The fascist planes are especially dreaded, and when they approach, all hope is lost. The efforts of the partisans seem to vanish, their commitment and their abilities become meaningless. ", especially the trench mortars that already wounded Lt. Henry ("he knew that they would die as soon as a mortar came up". No longer would the best soldier win, but the one with the biggest gun. The soldiers using those weapons are simple brutes, they lack "all conception of dignity" as Fernando remarked. Anselmo insisted, "We must teach them. We must take away their planes, their automatic weapons, their tanks, their artillery and teach them dignity".

The novel also contains imagery of soil and earth, most famously when Jordan has sex with María at the start of chapter thirteen and feels "the earth move out and away from under them" then afterwards asks María, "Did thee feel the earth move?", variants of which have become a cultural cliché, often used humorously.

## Literary significance and critical reaction

### Language

Since its publication, the prose style and dialogue in Hemingway's novel has been the source of controversy and some negative critical reaction. For example, Edmund Wilson, in a tepid review, noted the encumbrance of "a strange atmosphere of literary medievalism" in the relationship between Robert Jordan and Maria. This stems in part from a distinctive feature of the novel, namely Hemingway's extensive use of archaisms, implied transliterations and false friends to convey the foreign (Spanish) tongue spoken by his characters. Thus, Hemingway uses the archaic "thou' (particularly in its oblique and possessive form) to parallel the Spanish pronominal "tú" (familiar) and "Usted" (formal) forms. Additionally, much of the dialogue in the novel is an implied direct translation from Spanish, producing an often strained English equivalent. For example, Hemingway uses the construction "what passes that", which is an implied transliteration of the Spanish construction *que pasa*. This transliteration extends to the use of false friends, such as "rare" (from raro) instead of "strange" and "syndicate" (from sindicato) instead of trade union. In another odd stylistic variance, Hemingway referenced foul language (used with some frequency by different characters in the novel) with "unprintable" and "obscenity" in the dialogue, although foul language is used freely in Spanish even when its equivalent is censored in English (e.g. *joder, me cago*). The Spanish expression of exasperation *me cago en la leche* repeatedly recurs throughout the novel, translated by Hemingway as "I obscenity in the milk."

### Narrative style

The book is written in the third person limited omniscient narrative mode. The action and dialogue are punctuated by extensive thought sequences told from the viewpoint of Robert Jordan. The novel also contains thought sequences of other characters, including Pilar and Anselmo. The thought sequences are more extensive than in Hemingway's earlier fiction, notably *A Farewell to Arms*, and are an important narrative device to explore the principal themes of the novel.

In 1941 the Pulitzer Prize committee for letters unanimously recommended *For Whom the Bell Tolls* be awarded the prize for that year. The Pulitzer Board agreed; however, Nicholas Murray Butler, president of Columbia University at that time, overrode both and instead no award was given for letters that year.

Source (edited): "http://en.wikipedia.org/wiki/For_Whom_the_Bell_Tolls"

# Green Hills of Africa

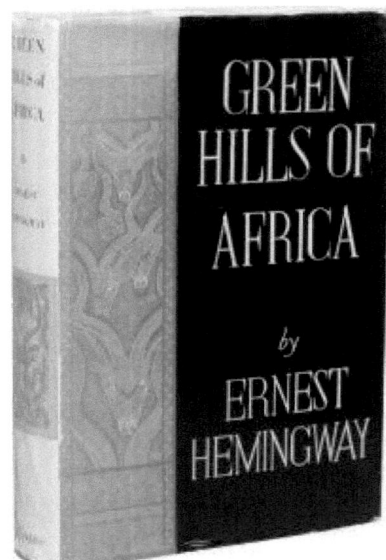

First edition cover

**Green Hills of Africa** is a 1935 work of nonfiction written by Ernest Hemingway (July 21, 1899 – July 2, 1961). Hemingway's second work of nonfiction, *Green Hills of Africa* is basically a journal of a month on safari he and his wife, Pauline Marie Pfeiffer, took in East Africa during December 1933. *Green Hills of Africa* is divided into four parts: Pursuit and Conversation, Pursuit Remembered, Pursuit and Failure, and Pursuit as Happiness, each of which plays a different role in the story.

## Synopsis

Much of narrative describes Hemingway's adventures hunting in East Africa, interspersed with ruminations about literature and authors. Generally the East African landscape Hemingway describes is in the region of Lake Manyara in Tanzania.

The book starts with Part 1 ("Pursuit and Conversation"), with Hemingway and a European expat in conversation about American writers. Relations between the white hunters and native trackers are described, as well as Hemingway's jealousy of the other hunters. Part 2 ("Pursuit Remembered") presents a flashback of hunting in northern Tanzania with a description of the Rift Valley and descriptions of how to field dress prey. Hemingway kills a rhino, but Karl kills a bigger one. The literary discussion moves to European writers such as Tolstoy, Flaubert, Stendhal, and Dostoevsky. In Part 3 ("Pursuit and Failure") the action returns to the present with Hemingway unlucky in hunting, unable to find a kudu he tracks. He moves to an untouched piece of country with the native trackers. In Part 4 ("Pursuit and Happiness") Hemingway and some of his trackers arrive at seemingly virgin country. There he kills a kudu bull with huge horns (52 inches). Back in the camp, he discovers that Karl killed a kudu with bigger horns. He complains that Karl is a terrible hunter with infinite luck. On the last day he learns that many of the guides consider him a brother.

## Background and publication history

*Green Hills of Africa* (1935) initially appeared in serialization in Scribner's Magazine, and was published in 1935. An autobiographical journal of his 1933 trip to Africa, Hemingway presents the subject of big game hunting in a nonfiction form in *Green Hills of Africa*. The serialization occurred from May to November of 1935. The book was published on 25 October 1935 to a first edition print-run of 10,500 copies.

## Reception

Ernest Hemingway poses with kudu Africa, February 1934. JFK Library

*Green Hills of Africa* initially got a cool reception. Writing for *The New York Times*, critic John Chamberlain claimed: "Green Hills of Africa" is not one of the major Hemingway works. Mr. Hemingway has so simplified his method that all his characters talk the lingo perfected in "The Sun Also Rises," whether these characters are British, Austrian, Arabian, Ethiopian or Kikuyu." However, two days later, writing for the same newspaper, critic C. G. Poore hailed *The Green Hills of Africa* as "the best-written story of big-game hunting anywhere I have read. And more than that. It's a book about people in unacknowledged conflict and about the pleasures of travel and the pleasures of drinking and war and peace and writing." Despite the better review, Hemingway said the book critics "killed" the book. He went into a deep depression, and said he was " 'ready to blow my lousy head off' ". Within a few months he was ready to blame the corrupting influence of the wealthy women in his life—his wife Pauline and his mistress Jane Mason. The result of his bitterness were two stories about Africa: "The Short Happy Life of Francis Macomber" and "The Snows of Kilimanjaro", that featured husbands married to domineering women.

## Literary analysis

The foreword of *Green Hills of Africa* immediately identifies this as a work of nonfiction that should be compared with similar works of fiction:

Unlike many novels, none of the characters or incidents in this book is imaginary. Any one not finding sufficient love interest is at liberty, while reading it, to insert whatever love interest he or she may have at the time. The writer has attempted to write an absolutely true book to see whether the shape of a country and the pattern of a month's action can, if truly presented, compete with a work of the imagination.

The book is well known today for a line that has nearly nothing to do with its subject. This quote is frequently used as evidence that *The Adventures of Huckleberry Finn* is The Great American Novel:

The good writers are Henry James, Stephen Crane, and Mark Twain. That's not the order they're good in. There is no order for good writers.... All modern American literature comes from one book by Mark Twain called *Huckleberry Finn*. If you read it you must stop where the Nigger Jim is stolen from the boys. That is the real end. The rest is just cheating. But it's the best book we've had. All American writing comes from that. There was nothing before. There has been nothing as good since.

One episode in *Green Hills of Africa* is Hemingway's conversation with the Austrian hunter Kandisky, whom Hemingway stops to help when Kandisky's truck breaks down. After initially trading opinions on German writers like Rainer Maria Rilke and Thomas Mann, Hemingway and the Austrian later discuss American literature over dinner, and it turns out that one of the few American writers Hemingway approves of is Henry James, whom he mentions twice.

Specifically, Hemingway says: "The good American writers are Henry James, Stephen Crane, and Mark Twain" and adds later that "Henry James wanted to make money. He never did, of course". Intermixed with these comments on James, Crane, and Twain are Hemingway's views of American writers in general, most of whom, he says, came to a bad end. When Kandisky asks about himself Hemingway tells him, "I am interested in other things. I have a good life but I must write because if I do not write a certain amount I do not enjoy the rest of my life." When asked what he wants, Hemingway replies, "To write as well as I can and learn as I go along. At the same time I have my life which I enjoy and which is a damned good life."

Source (edited): "http://en.wikipedia.org/wiki/Green_Hills_of_Africa"

## Hills Like White Elephants

"**Hills Like White Elephants**" is a short story by Ernest Hemingway. It was first published in the 1927 collection *Men Without Women*.

### Plot summary

The story takes place at a train station in the Ebro River valley of Spain. The year is not given, but is almost certainly contemporary to the composition (1920s). This particular day is oppressively hot and dry, and the scenery in the valley is barren and ugly for the most part. The two main characters are a man (referred to only as "the American") and his female companion, whom he calls Jig.

While waiting for the train to Madrid, the American and Jig drink beer and a liquor called *Anís del Toro*, which Jig compares to liquorice. Their conversation is mundane at first, but quickly drifts to the subject of an operation which the American is attempting to convince Jig to undergo. Though it is never made explicit in the text, it is made clear (through phrases of dialogue such as "It's just to let the air in" and "But I don't want anybody but you," among numerous context clues) that Jig is pregnant and that the procedure in question is an abortion.

After posing arguments to which the American is largely unresponsive, Jig next assents to the operation, while saying: "I don't care about me." However, he then responds, "You've got to realize that I don't want you to do it if you don't want to." He continues, "I'm perfectly willing to go through with it if it means anything to you." She attempts to drop the subject, but the American persists as if still unsure of Jig's intentions and mental state. She insists, "Would you please please ... please stop talking?" He is silent a while, and repeats, "But I don't want you to," and adds, "I don't care anything about it." She interjects, "I'll scream."

The barmaid comes out through the beaded curtains with two glasses of beer and puts them down on the damp felt pads. She notes, "The train comes in five minutes." Jig was distracted, but then smiles brightly at the woman and thanks her.

He leaves the table and carries their bags to the opposing platform, but still no sight of the train in the distance. He walks back through the station, and everyone else is still waiting reasonably for the train. Pausing at the bar, he drinks another Anis, alone, before rejoining Jig. He then asks her, "Do you feel better?" She again smiles at him, "I feel fine. There's nothing wrong with me. I feel fine." The story ends.

### Symbolism and setting

Jig's reference to white elephants could be in regard to the baby. The American could see the baby as a white elephant and not want to raise it because of the cost, while Jig could see the child as an extraordinary addition to her mundane life of drinking and mindless traveling.

"Hills Like White Elephants" shows Hemingway's use of iceberg theory or theory of omission: a message is presented through a story's subtext; for instance, in "Hills Like White Elephants" the word 'abortion' is never uttered although the male character seems to be attempting to convince his girlfriend to have an abortion.

The title of the story, "Hills Like White Elephants," is an allegory of the innocence of what seemed to be but is not (Jig's lust towards an American man) from Jig's perspective in regards to her affair with a man who simply sees the pleasure in being with her in the flesh. Innocence is revealed when Jig orders a drink that she has never had before, and does not know the taste of. This is an allegory which develops into mixed feelings as the story unfolds. Jig muses, "Everything tastes of licorice. Especially all the things you've waited so long for, like absinthe." This clearly reflects that, in her innocence, she is confused. She does go on to express his immorality towards her as she expresses that everything to her tastes like licorice. This reflects her intoxication which goes beyond the physical, as he abused her physically, and also emotionally. The American answers, "Oh cut it out", which is a pun intended as a nod toward abortion, and goes on saying, "Well, let's try and have a fine time."

The title of the story refers to an aspect of its setting which is symbolically important in many ways. Jig draws a simple simile by describing the hills across the desolate valley as looking like white elephants. The implication is that, just as Jig thinks the hills in the distance look like white elephants, the American views the couple's unborn child as an approaching obstacle, a hindrance to the status quo or status quo ante. To avoid this impending responsibility, he attempts to manipulate Jig into having an abortion by presenting the operation as a simple procedure that is in her best interests, a panacea for all that is ailing her and troubling their relationship.

Furthermore, this symbolism combined with Jig's question "That's all we do, isn't it--look at things and try new drinks" and her statement that even exciting new things she has waited a long time to try, like absinthe (sometimes valued as an aphrodisiac), merely end up "tasting like licorice," implies that the couple's perpetually ambling, hedonistic circus-like lifestyle has become something of a metaphorical white elephant to her. It appears that she seeks more stability and permanence in life; "It isn't ours anymore," she states of the carefree lifestyle she and the American have been pursuing from one hotel to the next.

The symbolism of the hills and the big white elephant can be thought of as the image of the swollen breasts and abdomen of a pregnant woman, and to the prenatal dream of the mother of the future Buddha in which a white elephant (in this case, a symbol of prestigious leadership) presents her with a lotus flower, a symbol of fertility.

The reference to the white elephants may also bear a connection to the baby as 'a valuable possession of which its owner cannot dispose and whose cost (particularly cost of upkeep) is out of proportion to its usefulness.'

Apart from the eponymous hills, other parts of the setting provide symbolism which expresses the tension and conflict surrounding the couple. The train tracks form a dividing line between the barren expanse of land stretching toward the hills on one side and the green, fertile farmland on the other, symbolizing the choice faced by each of the main characters and their differing interpretations of the dilemma of pregnancy. Jig focuses on the landscape during the conversation, rarely making eye contact with the American.

At the end of the story, the American takes the initiative to pick up the couple's luggage and port it to the "other tracks" on the opposite side of the station, symbolizing his sense of primacy in making the decision to give up their child and betraying his insistence to Jig that the decision is entirely in her hands.

Some have noted the similarity of the two damp felt pads, on the table, and nursing pads. Meanwhile, Jig is the one who is pregnant, and in the end, she concludes, "There's nothing wrong with me. I feel fine."

**Dialogue**

"They look like white elephants," she said.
"I've never seen one," the man drank this beer.
"No, you wouldn't have."
"I might have," the man said. "Just because you say I wouldn't have doesn't prove anything."
The girl looked at the bead curtain. "They've painted something on it," she said. "What does it say?"
"Anis del Toro. It's a drink."
"Could we try it?"

The reader must interpret their dialogue and body language to infer their backgrounds and their attitudes with respect to the situation at hand, and their attitudes toward one another. From the outset of the story, the contentious nature of the couple's conversation indicates resentment and unease. Some critics have written that the dialogue is a distillation of the contrasts between stereotypical male and female relationship roles: in the excerpt above, for instance, Jig draws the comparison with white elephants, but the hyper-rational male immediately denies it, dissolving the bit of poetry into objective realism with "I've never seen one." She also asks his permission to order a drink. Throughout the story, Jig is distant; the American is rational. While the American attempts to frame the fetus as the source of the couple's discontent with life and one another, the tone and pattern of dialogue indicate that there may be deeper problems with the relationship than the purely circumstantial. This ambiguity leaves a good deal of room for interpretation; while most critics have espoused relatively straightforward interpretations of the dialogue (with Jig as the dynamic character, traveling reluctantly from rejection to acceptance of the idea of an abortion), a few have argued for alternate scenarios based upon the same dialogue.

Source (edited): "http://en.wikipedia.org/wiki/Hills_Like_White_Elephants"

# In Another Country

"**In Another Country**" is a short story by American author Ernest Hemingway.

It is about an ambulance corps member in Milan during World War I. Although unnamed, he is assumed to be "Nick" a character Hemingway made to represent himself. He has an injured knee and visits a hospital daily for rehabilitation. There the "machines" are used to speed the healing, with the doctors making much of the miraculous new technology. They show pictures to the wounded of injuries like theirs healed by the machines, but the war-hardened soldiers are portrayed as skeptical, perhaps justifiably so.

As the narrator walks through the streets with fellow soldiers, the townspeople hate them openly because they are officers. Their oasis from this treatment is Cafe Cova, where the waitresses are very patriotic.

When the fellow soldiers admire the protagonist's medal, they learn that he is American, ipso facto not having to face the same struggles in order to achieve the medal, and no longer view him as an equal, but still recognize him as a friend against the outsiders. The protagonist accepts this, since he feels that they have done far more to earn their medals than he has. Later on, a major who is friends with the narrator, in an angry fit tells Nick he should never get married, it being only a way to set one up for hurt. It is later revealed that the major's wife had suddenly and unexpectedly died. The major is depicted as far more grievously wounded, with a hand withered to the size of a baby's hand, and Hemingway memorably describes the withered hand being manipulated by a machine which the major dismisses as a "damn thing." But the major seems even more deeply wounded by the loss of his wife.

It is also implied this entire episode is a dream, by subtle references to night time and searching for needed light. It is reminiscent of Dante's Inferno.

Source (edited): "http://en.wikipedia.org/wiki/In_Another_Country"

## *In Our Time* (book)

*In Our Time* is a collection of short stories by Ernest Hemingway. Each chapter consists of a vignette that in some way relates to the following short story. It was published in 1925, and marked Ernest Hemingway's American debut. It contains several well-known Hemingway works, including the Nick Adams stories "Indian Camp," "The Doctor and the Doctor's Wife," "The Three Day Blow," and "The Battler", and introduces readers to the hallmarks of the Hemingway style. "On the Quai at Smyrna" was first published as the introduction to the 1930 edition.

A year earlier in 1924, Hemingway published a much shorter book named *in our time* (in lower-case) in Paris. It consisted of just 32 pages and was published in a small edition of 170 copies. *in our time* contained only the vignettes later used as interchapters for *In Our Time*, though some of these vignettes, like "A Very Short Story" and "The Revolutionist," were treated as full short stories in the later collection.

The title comes from the English Book of Common Prayer: "give us peace in our time, O Lord." This origin was first suggested by Ezra Pound and then later confirmed by Hemingway.

At the time of its publication, the book was recognized as a significant development in prose fiction, for its spare language and oblique depiction of the psychological states of the characters portrayed. Retrospectively, *In Our Time* is viewed as the beginning of Hemingway's highly influential style, which would make an indelible mark on 20th century prose fiction.

### List of stories

- "On the Quai at Smyrna"
- "Indian Camp"
- "The Doctor and the Doctor's Wife"
- "The End of Something"
- "The Three-Day Blow"
- "The Battler"
- "A Very Short Story"
- "Soldier's Home"
- "The Revolutionist"
- "Mr. And Mrs. Elliot"
- "Cat in the Rain"
- "Out of Season"
- "Cross-Country Snow"
- "My Old Man"
- "Big Two-Hearted River"

Source (edited): "http://en.wikipedia.org/wiki/In_Our_Time_(book)"

# Indian Camp

Hemingway's 1923 passport photo taken a year before the publication of "Indian Camp"

"**Indian Camp**" is a short story written by Ernest Hemingway. The story was first published in 1924 in Ford Madox Ford's literary magazine *transatlantic review* in Paris, and republished by Boni & Liveright in 1925 in the American edition of Hemingway's first volume of short stories *In Our Time*. "Indian Camp" is the first of Hemingway's stories to feature the semi-autobiographical character Nick Adams—a child in this story—which is told from his point-of-view.

In the story, Nick Adams' father, a country doctor, has been summoned to an Indian camp to deliver a baby, with Nick and his uncle going along with him. At the camp, the father is forced to perform an emergency caesarean section using a jack-knife, with Nick as his assistant. Afterward, the woman's husband is discovered dead, having fatally slit his throat during the operation. The story is important because it shows the emergence of Hemingway's understated style and use of counterpoint. "Indian Camp" has themes such as childbirth and fear of death, which permeate much of his subsequent work. When *In Our Time* was published the quality of writing was noted and praised; scholars consider "Indian Camp" an important story in the Hemingway canon.

## Plot summary

The story begins as young Nick Adams, his father and his uncle, row a boat across a lake to an Indian camp. Nick's physician father has been summoned to deliver a child for a woman who has been in labor for days. At the camp, they find the woman in a cabin lying on the bottom of a bunkbed; above, lies her husband with an injured foot. While Nick holds a basin, his father performs a Caesarian operation with a jack-knife. After the baby's delivery, Nick's father realizes the woman's husband has fatally slit his throat with a straight-edged razor and is covered with blood. Nick is sent out of the cabin to discover his uncle gone. The story ends with Nick and his father, in the boat, on the lake, rowing away from the camp. Nick asks his father why the woman's husband killed himself, as he silently tells himself he will never die.

## Background

In the early 1920s, Hemingway and his wife Hadley lived in Paris where he was foreign correspondent for the Toronto Star. When Hadley became pregnant they returned to Toronto. The story was written a few months after John Hemingway was born on 10 October 1923. Hemingway biographer Kenneth Lynn suggests that the experience inspired Hemingway to write the story. Hemingway was on a train, returning from New York to Toronto, when Hadley went into labor. Lynn believes Hemingway was likely terrified Hadley would not survive the birth, and he became "beside himself with fear ... about the extent of her suffering and swamped by a sense of helplessness at the realization that he would probably arrive too late to be of assistance to her".

In the story, Nick Adams' father, the doctor, who is portrayed as "professionally cool," is based on Hemingway's own father, Clarence Hemingway. Hemingway's paternal uncle, George, appears in the story, and is treated unsympathetically.

## Publication history

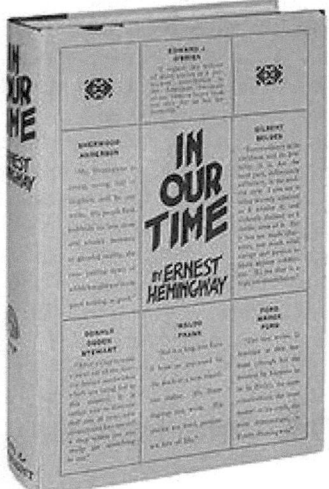

"Indian Camp" was published by Boni and Liveright in the short story collection *In Our Time*, shown here in first edition with dustwrapper

"Indian Camp" began as a 29 page untitled manuscript that Hemingway cut to 7 pages; initially the story was titled "One Night Last Summer". The original manuscript included a section that would eventually be published posthumously as "Three Shots". In 1924, the story was first published in Paris in Ford Madox Ford's literary magazine *transatlantic review*, edited by Ezra Pound. "Indian Camp" was placed in a section titled "Works in Progress" that included a piece from James Joyce's manuscript *Finnegan's Wake*. "Indian Camp" was republished a year later, on 5 October 1925 by Boni & Liveright, in an expanded edition titled *In Our Time*. The initial print-run was 1335 copies.

"Indian Camp" was later included in Hemingway's collection *The Fifth Column and the First Forty-Nine Stories* published in October 1938. Two collections of short stories published after Hemingway's death included "Indian Camp": *The Nick Adams Stories* (1972)

and *The Complete Short Stories of Ernest Hemingway: The Finca Vigía Edition* (1987). *The Nick Adams Stories* (1972), edited by Philip Young, included the story fragment titled "Three Shots" that Hemingway originally cut from "Indian Camp."

## Writing style

Carlos Baker maintains that Hemingway learned in his short stories how to "get the most from the least, how to prune language how to multiply intensities, and how to tell nothing but the truth in a way that allowed for telling more than the truth". The style is known as the iceberg theory because in Hemingway's writing the hard facts float above water; the supporting structure, complete with symbolism, operates out-of-sight. Jackson Benson believes Hemingway used autobiographical details to work as framing devices to write about life in general—not only about his life. The concept of the iceberg theory is sometimes referred to as the "theory of omission." Hemingway believed the writer could describe one thing though an entirely different thing occurs below the surface. Tetlow believes in this early story Hemingway showed little concern for character development by simply placing the character in his surroundings, with the use of descriptive detail such as a screaming woman, men smoking tobacco, and an infected wound lending a sense of veracity.

"Indian Camp" is constructed in three parts: the first places Nick and his father on a dark lake; the second takes place in the squalid and cramped cabin amid terrifying action; and the third shows Nick and his father back on the lake—bathed in sunlight. Hemingway's use of counterpoint in his fiction is evident in "Indian Camp", as at the end Nick trails his hand in the lake water that "felt warm in the sharp chill of the morning". Paul Strong believes the deleted section provided context and counterpoint to the plot. For example, in "Three Shots" Nick is alone in the "stillness of the night" whereas in "Indian Camp" the middle scene is crowded with people. Strong believes it is likely Hemingway eliminated those scenes to create counterpoint and unity between "Indian Camp" and the next Nick Adams story "The Doctor and the Doctor's Wife". Paul Smith writes that the elimination of the material later renamed and published as "Three Shots" serves to focus on the immediacy of the central point of the story: the initiation rituals of life and death familiar to the residents of the Indian camp, but alien to young Nick. Unable to express his feelings in fullness, in the end, as he trails his water "he felt quite sure that he would never die".

## Themes and genre

### Initiation

The story is an initiation story, in which the child Nick is initiated to the adult world of childbirth and death. Nick's father (Dr. Adams) introduces his son to sexuality, childbirth, and unintentionally to violent death—for Nick the two become inextricably interwoven. Wendolyn Tetlow maintains that in "Indian Camp" sexuality culminates in "butchery-style" birth and bloody death, and that Nick's anxiety is manifested when he must turn away from the events in the cabin. The story reaches a climax with Nick's "heightened awareness" of evil, which Tetlow writes the child cannot assimilate, so he turns away. Later in the canoe, Nick denies death by asserting he will never die.

### Death

"Indian Camp" is about the fear of death. The pieces cut from the story highlight Nick's fear; the published version underscore Nick's fear in a less obvious manner. By introducing Nick Adams in "Indian Camp", biographer Philip Young writes that Hemingway's emphasis in "Indian Camp" was not so much on the woman who gives birth or the father who commits suicide, but on young Nick Adams, who witnesses these events and becomes a "badly scarred and nervous young man". Hemingway sets events in "Indian Camp" that shape the Adams persona. Young considers this single Hemingway story to hold the "master key" to "what its author was up to for some thirty-five years of his writing career". Critic Howard Hannum agrees. He believes the trauma of birth and suicide Hemingway paints in "Indian Camp" gave a leitmotif from which Nick could never escape—thereby providing Hemingway a framework of unity for the Nick Adams stories.

The question of the woman's husband, who commits suicide, is enigmatic. Paul Strong finds the arguments that the husband is driven to suicide by the wife's screaming to be problematic because the suicide occurs at the moment the screams are silenced. He writes the husband, perhaps, commits suicide because he is "driven frantic by his wife's pain, and perhaps his own". In his essay "Hemingway's Primitivism and 'Indian Camp'" Jeffrey Meyers writes that Hemingway was very clear about the husband's role, because in this story he was writing about a familiar subject—the experiences of his boyhood in Michigan. The young father's role is to "deflate the doctor", who finds victory in slicing open the woman's belly to deliver the infant, and to provide a counterpoint to the mother's strength and resilience. The father's suicide serves as a symbolic rejection of the white doctor whose skill is necessary but who brings with him destruction. In her paper "Screaming Through Silence: The Violence of Race in 'Indian Camp'" Amy Strong writes "Indian Camp" is about domination; the husband kills himself at the moment his wife is cut open by a white doctor. Strong sees the theme of domination on a variety of levels: the father dominates the son; the white outsiders dominate in the Indian camp; and the white doctor "has cut into the woman, like the early settlers leaving a gash in the tree."

The story also shows a belief in the innocence of childhood; Nick Adams believes he will live forever, be a child forever. Nick Adams is a character who sees his life "stretching ahead." However "Indian Camp" shows an early fascination with suicide, and conflict between fathers and sons. Young considers it "unavoidable" to focus on the fact that both the principals in the story—the father, based on Clarence Hemingway, and the boy, based on Hemingway himself—end up committing suicide. Kenneth Lynn agrees, and points out the irony to modern readers: both characters in "that boat on the lake would one day do away with themselves", referring to Hemingway's father's suicide in the late 1920s, and Hemingway's in 1961.

**Autobiographical elements**

Meyers claims the story is not autobiographical though it is an early example of Hemingway's ability to tell stories "true to life." Of the relation between imagination and reality, Hemingway admitted that "Indian Camp" represents one of the stories in which his imagination makes a story seems real: "Everything good he'd ever written he'd made up ... Of course he'd never seen an Indian woman having a baby. That was what made it good." Jackson Benson writes in "Ernest Hemingway: The Life as Fiction and the Fiction as Life" that critics must ignore finding connections between the author's life and fiction and instead focus on the manner in which biographical events are transformed into art. He believes the events in a writer's life might have only a vague relationship to the fiction like a dream from which a drama emerges. Of Hemingway's earliest stories, Benson claims "his early fiction, his best, has often been compared to a nightmare".

**Reception and legacy**

Hemingway had received good reviews for his pamphlet of short stories published in 1924, titled *in our time*, in a small print-run from Ezra Pound's modernist series through Three Mountains Press in Paris. At that time Edmund Wilson wrote, "that 'Hemingway's prose was of the first distinction'". Wilson's comments were sufficient to bring attention to the young writer.

"Indian Camp" received considerable praise. Ford Maddox Ford saw "Indian Camp" as an important early story by a young writer. When the story was first published in the mid-1920s, critics in the United States claimed Hemingway reinvigorated the short story by his use of declarative sentences and his crisp style. Hemingway admits *In Our Time* has a collection of stories with "pretty good unity" and generally critics agree.

Modern Hemingway scholars, such as Jackson Benson, rank "Indian Camp" as one of Hemingway's "greatest short stories," a story that is described as "best known", "violent" and "dramatic". In 1992, Frederick Busch wrote in *The New York Times* that Hemingway had gone out of fashion. His anti-semitism, racism, violence and attitude toward women and homosexuals made him a politically incorrect writer; but he turned violence into art unlike any other American writer of his time by showing that "the making of art is a matter of life or death, no less". Busch writes that Hemingway's attitude is evident as early as 1924 in the stories of *In Our Time*—characters in his fiction either faced life or chose death, a choice shown most starkly in "Indian Camp". The saving of a life in "Indian Camp" is at the center of Hemingway's fiction, Busch writes, and what continues to give his fiction power, decades after the author himself chose death by suicide in 1961.

Source (edited): "http://en.wikipedia.org/wiki/Indian_Camp"

## *Islands in the Stream* (novel)

*Islands in the Stream* (1970) was the first of the published posthumous work by Ernest Hemingway (July 21, 1899 – July 2, 1961).

The book was originally intended to revive Hemingway's reputation after the negative reviews of *Across the River and Into the Trees*. He began writing it in 1950 and advanced greatly through 1951. The work, rough but seemingly finished, was found by Mary Hemingway from among 332 different works Hemingway left behind after his death.

*Islands in the Stream* was meant to encompass three stories to illustrate different stages in the life of its main character, Thomas Hudson. The three different parts of the novel were originally to be entitled "The Sea When Young", "The Sea When Absent" and "The Sea in Being". These titles were changed, however, into what are now its three acts: "Bimini", "Cuba", and "At Sea".

**Background**

Early in 1950 Hemingway started work on a "sea trilogy", to consist of three sections: "The Sea When Young" (set in Bimini); "The Sea When Absent" (set in Havana); and "The Sea in Being". The latter was published in 1952 as *The Old Man and the Sea*. He also wrote an unpublished "Sea-Chase" story which his wife and editor combined with the stories about the islands, renamed *Islands in the Stream* and published in 1970.

**Plot**

The first act, "Bimini", begins with an introduction to the character of Thomas Hudson, a classic Hemingway stoic male figure. Hudson is a renowned American painter who finds tranquility on the island of Bimini, in the Bahamas, a far cry from his usual adventurous lifestyle. Hudson's strict routine of work is interrupted when his three sons arrive for the summer and is the setting for most of the act. Also introduced in this act is the character of Roger Davis, one of Hudson's oldest friends. Though similar to Hudson, by struggling with an unmentioned internal conflict, Davis seems to act as a more dynamic and outgoing image of Hudson's character. The act ends with Hudson receiving news of the death of his two youngest children soon after they leave the island.

"Cuba" takes place soon thereafter during the second World War, where we are introduced to an older and more distant Hudson who has just received news of his oldest (and last) son's death in the war. This second act introduces us to a more cynical and introverted Hudson who spends his days on the island drinking heavily and doing naval reconnaissance for the US Army.

"At Sea", the final act, ends leaving the reader to assume Hudson dies after being wounded in a shoot out which capped a pursuit (by him and a team of irregulars) of German sailors whose U-boat was presumably sunk in the Gulf Stream, although the ending is slightly ambiguous. Hudson becomes intent on finding the fleeing Germans after he finds they massacred an entire village to cover their escape. In this last act Hudson stops questioning the death of his children. This chapter rings heavily with influences of Hemingway's earlier work *For Whom the Bell Tolls*.

Source (edited): "http://en.wikipedia.org/wiki/Islands_in_the_Stream_(novel)"

## *Men Without Women* (short story collection)

*Men Without Women* (1927) is a collection of short stories written by American author Ernest Hemingway (July 21, 1899 – July 2, 1961). The volume consists of fourteen stories, ten of which had been previously published in magazines. The story subjects include bullfighting, infidelity, divorce and death. "The Killers", "Hills Like White Elephants" and "In Another Country" are considered to be among Hemingway's best work.

In a letter to F. Scott Fitzgerald dated September 1927, Hemingway tells that he originally wanted to find another title from the Book of Ecclesiastes (source of *The Sun Also Rises*) but, upon borrowing an Anglican vicar's bible, discovered that Rudyard Kipling and others had mined all potential biblical quotations, leaving him to come up with *Men Without Women* off the cuff.

### Stories

- "The Undefeated"
- "In Another Country"
- "Hills Like White Elephants"
- "The Killers"
- "Che Ti Dice La Patria?"
- "Fifty Grand"
- "A Simple Enquiry"
- "Ten Indians"
- "A Canary for One"
- "An Alpine Idyll"
- "A Pursuit Race"
- "Today is Friday"
- "Banal Story"
- "Now I Lay Me"

Source (edited): "http://en.wikipedia.org/wiki/Men_Without_Women_(short_story_collection)"

## Nick Adams (character)

**Nick Adams** is a fictional character, the protagonist of two dozen short stories by American author Ernest Hemingway, written in the 1920s and 30s. Adams is partly inspired by Hemingway's own experiences, from his summers in Northern Michigan to his service in the Red Cross ambulance corps in World War I.

Most of these stories were collected in a 1972 book titled *The Nick Adams Stories*. They are, for the most part, stories of initiation and adolescence. Taken as a whole, as in *The Nick Adams Stories*, they chronicle a young man's coming of age in a series of linked episodes. The stories are grouped according to major time periods in Nick's life.

### Nick Adams Stories

#### The Northern Woods

- "Three Shots"
- "Indian Camp"
- "The Doctor and the Doctor's Wife"
- "Ten Indians"
- "The Indians Moved Away"

#### On His Own

- "The Light of the World"
- "The Battler"
- "The Killers"
- "The Last Good Country"
- "Crossing the Mississippi"

~ age 16-20, late adolescence

#### War

- "Night Before Landing"
- "'Nick sat against the wall ...'"
- "Now I Lay Me"
- "A Way You'll Never Be"
- "In Another Country"

#### A Soldier Home

- "Big Two-Hearted River"
- "The End of Something"
- "The Three-Day Blow"
- "Summer People"

#### Company of Two

- "Wedding Day"
- "On Writing"
- "An Alpine Idyll"
- "Cross-Country Snow"
- "Fathers and Sons"

A scene from *The Killers*; Phil Brown as Nick Adams is seated in the left foreground.

### In film

Outside of film adaptations of "The Killers", the Nick Adams stories have never been fully portrayed on screen; however, in most of the previously mentioned film adaptations, the character is included, nevertheless.

In Robert Siodmak's 1946 adaptation, the character, though minor, is played by Phil Brown (better known as Uncle Owen in *Star Wars*); in the 1956 Andrei Tarkovsky collaborative student film, which sticks closely to Ernest Hemingway's original text, Adams is played by Yuli Fait. The Don Siegel-directed 1964 production is a radically

## Now I Lay Me

"**Now I Lay Me**" is a short story by American author Ernest Hemingway.

The story is about Nick Adams, one of Hemingway's recurring characters, forcing himself to stay awake at night in an army tent during World War I. He is afraid that if he goes to sleep in the dark his soul will escape him. Nick is experiencing shell-shock from when he was bombed during a night raid. During the raid Nick severely injured his head. From then on he was afraid to go to sleep at night.

Source (edited): "http://en.wikipedia.org/wiki/Now_I_Lay_Me"

## Soldier's Home

"**Soldier's Home**" is a short story by Ernest Hemingway, first collected in *In Our Time* (1925).

### Characters

- Harold Krebs, a young man who is tormented from his experiences in the war. He eventually comes to the realization that he doesn't belong in his childhood home anymore and decides to leave.
- Harold's mother, a very religious woman. She tries to get her son out of his post-war trauma.
- Helen Krebs, Harold's younger sister. She plays indoor baseball and looks up to her brother.
- Harold's father, who is absent most of the time. He never makes a direct appearance in the story.

Source (edited): "http://en.wikipedia.org/wiki/Soldier%27s_Home"

## The Battler

"**The Battler**" is a short story written by Ernest Hemingway. It was included in the collection *In Our Time* (1925).

### Synopsis

Nick Adams is thrown from a moving train and finds temporary shelter in the form of a campfire. There, he meets an ex-boxer named Ad Francis. Francis takes an immediate liking to Adams, who he claims is a "tough kid."

Source (edited): "http://en.wikipedia.org/wiki/The_Battler"

## The Capital of the World (short story)

"**The Capital of the World**" is a short story by Ernest Hemingway. The story takes place in Madrid and follows Paco, a young waiter, and his desires to become a matador.

First published in *Esquire* in June 1936 as "The Horns of the Bull", it was changed to its present title in the short story collection *The Fifth Column and the First Forty-Nine Stories*, published in 1938.

Source (edited): "http://en.wikipedia.org/wiki/The_Capital_of_the_World_(short_story)"

## The Complete Short Stories of Ernest Hemingway

*The Complete Short Stories of Ernest Hemingway: The Finca Vigía Edition*, is a posthumous collection of Ernest Hemingway's (July 21, 1899 – July 2, 1961) short fiction, published in 1987. It contains the classic *First Forty-Nine Stories* plus a number of other works and a foreword by his sons.

Only a small handful of stories published during Hemingway's lifetime are not included in *The First Forty-Nine*. Five stories were written concerning the Spanish Civil War: "The Denunciation," "The Butterfly and the Tank," "Night Before Battle," "Under The Ridge," and "Nobody Ever Dies." Excepting "Nobody Ever Dies," these stories were collected in a posthumous 1969 volume with his play, entitled *The Fifth Column and Four Stories of the Spanish Civil War*. Chicote's bar and the Hotel Florida in Madrid are recurrent settings in these stories.

In March 1951, *Holiday* magazine published two of Hemingway's short children's stories, "The Good Lion" and "The Faithful Bull." Two more short stories were to appear in Hemingway's lifetime: "Get A Seeing-Eyed Dog" and "A Man Of The World," both in the December 20, 1957 issue of the *Atlantic Monthly*.

The seven unpublished stories included in *The Complete Short Stories of Ernest Hemingway: The Finca Vigía Edition* are "A Train Trip," "The Porter," "Black Ass at the Cross Roads," "Landscape with Figures," "I Guess Everything Reminds You of Something," "Great News from the Mainland," and "The Strange Country."

In addition, this volume includes "An African Story," which was derived from the unfinished and heavily edited posthumous novel *The Garden of Eden* (1986), and two parts of the 1937 novel *To Have And Have Not*, "One Trip Across" (*Cosmopolitan,* May 1934) and "The Tradesman's Return" (*Esquire,* February 1936), in their original magazine versions.

The collection is not, despite the title, complete. After Hemingway's suicide, Scribner put out a collection called *The Nick Adams Stories* (1972) which contains many old stories already collected in *The First Forty-Nine* as well as some previously unpublished pieces (much of it material that Hemingway clearly rejected). From the new material, only "The Last Good Country" (part of an unfinished novella) and "Summer People" are included in this volume.

For the Hemingway short fiction completist, some readers may turn to the Everyman's Library *The Collected Stories* (1995), published in the UK only, and introduced by James Fenton. Eschewing the pieces collected in *The Garden of Eden* and *To Have and Have Not,* Fenton's collection includes all the pieces from *The Nick Adams Stories* as well as a number of pieces of juvenilia and pre-Paris stories.

### Part I: First Forty-Nine Stories
- **Stories from *The Fifth Column and the First Forty-Nine Stories* (1938)**
  - The Short Happy Life of Francis Macomber (1936)
  - The Capital of the World
  - The Snows of Kilimanjaro
  - Old Man at the Bridge (1938)
- **From *Three Stories and Ten Poems* (1923)**
  - Up in Michigan (1923, revised 1938)
- ***In Our Time* (1925 and 1930)**
  - On the Quai at Smyrna
  - Indian Camp
  - The Doctor and the Doctor's Wife
  - The End of Something
  - The Three-Day Blow
  - The Battler
  - A Very Short Story
  - Soldier's Home
  - The Revolutionist
  - Mr. And Mrs. Elliot
  - Cat in the Rain
  - Out of Season
  - Cross-Country Snow
  - My Old Man
  - Big Two-Hearted River, Part I
  - Big Two-Hearted River, Part II
- ***Men Without Women* (1927)**
  - The Undefeated
  - In Another Country
  - Hills Like White Elephants
  - The Killers
  - Che Ti Dice La Patria?
  - Fifty Grand
  - A Simple Enquiry
  - Ten Indians
  - A Canary for One
  - An Alpine Idyll
  - A Pursuit Race
  - Today is Friday
  - Banal Story
  - Now I Lay Me
- ***Winner Take Nothing* (1933)**
  - After the Storm
  - A Clean, Well-Lighted Place
  - The Light of the World
  - God Rest You Merry, Gentlemen
  - The Sea Change
  - A Way You'll Never Be
  - The Mother of a Queen
  - One Reader Writes
  - Homage to Switzerland
  - A Day's Wait
  - A Natural History of the Dead
  - Wine of Wyoming
  - The Gambler, the Nun, and the Radio
  - Fathers and Sons

### Part II: Short Stories Published in Books or Magazines Subsequent to the *First Forty-Nine Stories*
- **From *To Have and Have Not***
  - One Trip Across (1934)
  - The Tradesman's Return (1936)
- **Uncollected stories published in Hemingway's lifetime**
  - The Denunciation (1938)
  - The Butterfly and the Tank (1938)
  - Night Before Battle (1939)
  - Under the Ridge (1939)
  - Nobody Ever Dies (1939)
  - The Good Lion (1951)
  - The Faithful Bull (1951)
  - Get a Seeing-Eyed Dog (1957)
  - A Man of the World (1957)
- **First published in *The Nick Adams Stories* (1972)**
  - Summer People
  - The Last Good Country
- **From *The Garden of Eden* (1986)**
  - An African Story

### Part III: Previously Unpublished Fiction
- A Train Trip
- The Porter
- Black Ass at the Crossroads
- Landscape with Figures
- I Guess Everything Reminds You of Something
- Great News from the Mainland
- The Strange Country

Source (edited): "http://en.wikipedia.org/wiki/The_Complete_Short_Stories_of_Ernest_Hemingway"

# The Dangerous Summer

**The Dangerous Summer** is a book written by Ernest Hemingway (July 21, 1899 – July 2, 1961), published in 1985, which describes the rivalry between bullfighters Luis Miguel Dominguín and his brother-in-law Antonio Ordóñez during the "dangerous summer" of 1959. It has been described as Hemingway's last book.

## Background

*The Dangerous Summer* is an edited version of a 75,000-word manuscript Hemingway wrote between October 1959 and May 1960 as an assignment from *LIFE Magazine*. Hemingway summoned his close friend Will Lang Jr. to come to Spain to deliver the story to *LIFE Magazine*. The book was edited from the original manuscript by his American publisher Charles Scribner's Sons. A 30,000-word extract from the script was published in three consecutive installments in *LIFE* during September 1960.

## Account of the season

The book charts the rise of Antonio Ordóñez (the son of Cayetano Ordóñez, whose exploits in the bull ring and fighting technique Hemingway had written about in *The Sun Also Rises*) across a season of bullfights during 1959. During a fight on May 13 in Aranjuez, Ordóñez is badly gored, but demonstrates his potential by remaining in the ring and killing the bull, a performance rewarded by trophies of both the bull's ears, its tail and a hoof.

In contrast, Luis Miguel Dominguín is a famous bullfighter returning to the ring after several years in retirement. Less naturally gifted than Ordóñez, his pride and self-belief draws him into an intense rivalry with the newcomer and the two meet in the ring several times during the season. Starting the season supremely confident, Dominguín is slowly humbled by this competition. Where Ordóñez displays breathtaking skill and artistry in the fights, performing highly dangerous classical passés, Dominguín often resorts to what Hemingway describes as "tricks", moves that look impressive to the crowd but that are actually much safer. Despite this, Dominguín is also gored badly at a fight in Valencia. Ordóñez is gored again at another fight shortly afterward. Less than a month later, the two bullfighters meet in the ring again for what Hemingway described as "one of the greatest bullfights I have ever seen" and "an almost perfect bullfight unmarred by any tricks." From the six bulls which they fight, the pair are awarded the trophies of ten ears, four tails and two hooves, an extraordinary feat. The final fight takes place in Bilbao with Dominguín's receiving a near-fatal goring and Ordóñez's showing his absolute mastery by performing the kill *recibiendo*, one of the oldest and most dangerous techniques. The kill takes three attempts, displaying Ordóñez's bravery and artistry which Hemingway likens to that of the legendary bullfighter Pedro Romero.

Source (edited): "http://en.wikipedia.org/wiki/The_Dangerous_Summer"

# The Doctor and the Doctor's Wife

"The Doctor and the Doctor's Wife" is a short story by Ernest Hemingway published in his 1925 volume of short stories *In Our Time*.

## Synopsis

A doctor hires a group of three Native Americans to clean up some logs on his property, and one of the workers casually asks him where he stole them from. The doctor gets angry, and the workers eventually leave.

After going back to his house, the doctor finds his wife and tells her what happened. He speculates that they started a fight with him to get out of doing the work, but she expresses doubt that anyone would do something like that.

The doctor leaves the house. He finds his son, Nick, reading a book outside and tells him that his mother would like to see him. However, Nick replies that he wants to go with his dad, and the doctor lets him.

Source (edited): "http://en.wikipedia.org/wiki/The_Doctor_and_the_Doctor%27s_Wife"

# The End of Something

"The End of Something" is a short story written by Ernest Hemingway. It was published in 1925 in the book *In Our Time*, a collection of short stories by Hemingway.

## Synopsis

In Hortons Bay, a town abandoned after the collapse of the logging industry, Nick Adams and his girlfriend, Marjorie, row a boat over to an island for a picnic. They spend most of the evening in silence. Then, Nick starts to express his reservations about their relationship. Marjorie asks him, "Isn't love fun anymore?" to which he says, "No." Marjorie leaves.

Before long, Bill ventures over to question him about what happened, but Nick angrily tells his friend to "go away."

## Themes

- The town – The town that they row past during the first part of the story is described as having passed its peak years ago, and it is now very worn-out and broken-looking. No one lives there anymore. It represents the state of Nick's and Marjorie's relationship.
- The fish – Marjorie, in an attempt to make conversation, comments that the fish are plentiful nearby. "But they won't bite," Nick replies. In this case, Nick is supposed to be a fish, and Marjorie the fisherman, trying to "lure" or "bait" Nick into marriage. However, Nick doesn't want to get married and won't "bite."
- Resolution – Despite, or maybe because of, the break-up, Nick is clearly depressed at the end of the story. He cannot escape his feeling of loss.

### Characters

- Nick Adams is a recurring character throughout this collection and other works by Hemingway.
- Marjorie
- Bill

Source (edited): "http://en.wikipedia.org/wiki/The_End_of_Something"

# The Fifth Column and the First Forty-Nine Stories

*The Fifth Column and the First Forty-Nine Stories* is an anthology of writings by Ernest Hemingway (July 21, 1899 – July 2, 1961) published in 1938. It contains Hemingway's only full-length play, *The Fifth Column*, and 49 short stories.

Many of the stories of the collection exist in other collections, including *In Our Time*, *Men Without Women*, *Winner Take Nothing* and *The Snows of Kilimanjaro*. Some of the collection's important stories include "Old Man at the Bridge", "On The Quai at Smyrna", "Hills Like White Elephants", "One Reader Writes", "The Killers" and "A Clean, Well-Lighted Place". While these stories are rather short, the book also includes some longer stories, among them "The Snows of Kilimanjaro" and "The Short Happy Life of Francis Macomber".

*The Fifth Column* is set during the Spanish Civil War. Its main character, Philip Rawlings, is an American-born secret agent for the Second Spanish Republic. The play was poorly received upon publication and has been overshadowed by many of the short stories in the anthology.

## Contents

*The Fifth Column and the First Forty-nine Stories* includes the stories from Hemingway's previous volumes of short stories *In Our Time*, *Men Without Women* and *Winner Take Nothing*. The book also includes Hemingway's Spanish Civil War play "The Fifth Column" as well as "The Short Happy Life of Francis Macomber", "The Snows of Kilimanjaro", "The Capital of the World" and "Old Man at the Bridge". It was published by Scribner's on 14 October 1938

### Short stories

- "The Short Happy Life of Francis Macomber"
- "The Capital of the World"
- "The Snows of Kilimanjaro"
- "Old Man at the Bridge"
- "Up in Michigan"
- "On the Quai at Smyrna"
- "Indian Camp"
- "The Doctor and the Doctor's Wife"
- "The End of Something"
- "The Three-Day Blow"
- "The Battler"
- "A Very Short Story"
- "Soldier's Home"
- "The Revolutionist"
- "Mr. and Mrs. Elliot"
- "Cat in the Rain"
- "Out of Season"
- "Cross-Country Snow"
- "My Old Man"
- "Big Two-Hearted River" (part 1)
- "Big Two-Hearted River" (part 2)
- "The Undefeated"
- "In Another Country"
- "Hills Like White Elephants"
- "The Killers"
- "Che Ti Dice La Patria?"
- "Fifty Grand"
- "A Simple Enquiry"
- "Ten Indians"
- "A Canary for One"
- "An Alpine Idyll"
- "A Pursuit Race"
- "Today is Friday"
- "Banal Story"
- "Now I Lay Me"
- "After the Storm"
- "A Clean, Well-Lighted Place"
- "The Light of the World"
- "God Rest You Merry, Gentlemen"
- "The Sea Change"
- "A Way You'll Never Be"
- "The Mother of a Queen"
- "One Reader Writes"
- "Homage to Switzerland"
- "A Day's Wait"
- "A Natural History of the Dead"
- "Wine of Wyoming"
- "The Gambler, the Nun, and the Radio"
- "Fathers and Sons"

Source (edited): "http://en.wikipedia.org/wiki/The_Fifth_Column_and_the_First_Forty-Nine_Stories"

# The Gambler, the Nun, and the Radio

"The Gambler, the Nun, and the Radio" is a short story by American writer Ernest Hemingway, which appears in the volume *The Snows of Kilimanjaro*. The original title was "Give us a Prescription, Doctor".

## Plot summary

The story takes place in a hospital run by a convent. The story focuses around a Mexican gambler named Cayetano, who was shot in a small town in Montana, a nun who aspires to be a saint and prays for everything or anything, and a writer named Mr. Frazer, who is ill, and constantly listens to the radio. To ease Cayetano's loneliness, the nun gets three Mexican musicians to come play for the people. One of the three musicians suggests that religion is the opium of the people, and distracts them from their ignorance. Frazer then tells how all people need opium to keep them from suffering too much. The nun had prayer, the doctors had humor, Cayetano had gambling and now the music of the three, and Frazer had his radio.

## Television adaptation

The story was dramatized for television in a one-hour adaptation shown in 1960. The television version starred Eleanor Parker, Richard Conte, and Charles

# The Garden of Eden

***The Garden of Eden*** is the second posthumously released novel of Ernest Hemingway (July 21, 1899 – July 2, 1961), published in 1986. Begun in 1946, Hemingway worked on the manuscript for the next 15 years, during which time he also wrote *The Old Man and the Sea*, *The Dangerous Summer*, *A Moveable Feast*, and *Islands in the Stream*.

## Plot summary

The novel is fundamentally the story of five months in the lives of David Bourne, an American writer, and his wife, Catherine. It is set mainly in the French Riviera, specifically in the Côte d'Azur, and in Spain. The story begins with their honeymoon in the Camargue. The Bournes soon meet a young woman named Marita, with whom they both fall in love, but only one can ultimately have her. David starts an affair with Marita, while his relationship with his wife deteriorates. The story continues until the apparent separation of David and Catherine.

## Major themes

The Garden of Eden indicates Hemingway's exploration of male-female relationships, shows an interest in androgynous characters, and "the reversal of gender roles."

Mellow argues the "ideas of sexual transference" did not become clear in Hemingway's fiction until he wrote *The Garden of Eden*. Catherine Bourne convinces David to dye his hair the color of hers, "so they are twins, summer-tanned and androgynous."

Yet while these notions are central to the novel's apparent plot, major analysis rests in noting that the story is a much more somber evocation of the modern condition. Here it depicts the lonely, fluctuating modern hero in David, and his inevitable entrance into an understanding of betrayal, fragmentation, and destruction. A critical image in this respect is the story of the elephant, which poignantly draws a parallel between the loss of innocence that came in his youth and the present degeneration of his shortly blissful marriage. Such imagery is also symbiotically strengthened in the context of the novel's title.

Another motif played out in the novel is the portrait of the artist—particularly, the artist that is Hemingway. Hemingway often slips into passages that attempt to convey the process of writing or creating powerful works of art. And at one point, he has David telling himself, "[b]e careful ...it is all very well for you to write simply and the simpler the better. But do not start to think so damned simply. Know how complicated it is and then state it simply."

## Background

Hemingway biographer James Mellow argues the genesis of the story began during Hemingway's honeymoon with his second wife, Pauline Pfeiffer, and shortly after his divorce from Hadley Richardson. The male protagonist's depiction as a young writer, and the woman's depiction as "attractive, exciting, wealthy" mirrored the days spent in Le Grau-du-Roi with Pauline.

Hemingway began *The Garden of Eden* in 1946 and wrote 800 pages. The novel was published posthumously in a much-abridged form in 1986. For fifteen years he continued to work on the novel which remained uncompleted. When published in 1986, the novel had 30 chapters and 70,000 words. The publisher's note explains that cuts were made to the novel, and according to biographers, Hemingway had achieved 48 chapters and 200,000 words. Scribner's removed as much as two-thirds of the extant manuscript and one long subplot.

## Publication

*The Garden of Eden*, Hemingway's ninth novel, was published in 1986, a quarter century after his death. Scribner's published the novel in May 1986 with a first print-run of 100,000 copies.

## Cover

The original cover for "The Garden of Eden" features the Juan Gris painting "Woman With A Basket."

## Reception

The publication of *The Garden of Eden* is controversial because of the editing done to the manuscript. Susan Seitz argues that in this novel Hemingway was forging a new direction in his fiction which was lost in the editing process. She believes the editing to have been substandard, with "substantial cuts of lines, scenes, and whole chapters, the addition of manuscript material that Hemingway had discarded, and transposed scenes and dialogue." The result, she claims, does not "represent Hemingway's intentions in these works as he left them."

## Film adaptation

A film adaptation of *The Garden of Eden* was released in 2008 at the RomaCinemaFest and had a limited investors' screening in the UK. Screen International dubbed the film "a boundaries-breaking erotic drama." The film went on general release in select theaters in December 2010. The ensemble cast featured Jack Huston, Mena Suvari, Caterina Murino, Richard E. Grant, and Carmen Maura. It was directed by John Irvin. The adaptation was by James Scott Linville, former editor of *The Paris Review*. In March 2011, the film went on sale on iTunes and with other vendors.

Source (edited): "http://en.wikipedia.org/wiki/The_Garden_of_Eden"

# The Killers (short story)

"**The Killers**" is a short story by Ernest Hemingway. It first appeared to the public in 1927 in *Scribner's Magazine*. How much Hemingway received for the literary piece is unknown, but some sources state it was $200. Historians have some documents showing that the working title of the piece was "The Matadors". After its appearance in *Scribner's*, the story was published in *Men Without Women, Snows of Kilimanjaro* and *The Nick Adams Stories*. The writer's depiction of the human experience, his use of satire, and the everlasting themes of death, friendship, and the purpose of life have contributed to make "The Killers" one of Hemingway's most famous and frequently anthologized short stories.

The story features Nick Adams, a famous Hemingway character from his short stories. In this story, Hemingway shows Adams crossing over from teenager to adult. The basic plot of the story involves a pair of criminals that enter a restaurant seeking to kill a boxer, a Swede named Ole Andreson, who is hiding out for reasons unknown (probably for not cooperating with the proposed rigging of a fight).

In 1984, the anthology *Hemingway at Oak Park High* was published by Oak Park and River Forest High School, and included short works that Hemingway had written for his school newspaper and literary magazine. One of the stories, "A Matter of Colour", involves the plot of a boxing manager to have a man named Swede hide behind a curtain and hit an opponent during a bout. Swede somehow fails, and in retaliation, the boxing manager puts out a contract on his life.

## Summary

The story takes place in a suburb of Chicago called Summit during the 1910s. Two hit men, Max and Al, walk into Henry's lunch-room, which is run by George, and order something off the menu that is not available and have to settle for pork and eggs. Al goes into the kitchen and ties up Nick Adams, a recurring character in Hemingway's stories, and Sam the black cook. Max and George soon have a conversation, which reveals that the two men are there to kill Ole Andreson, a Swedish boxer, for a "friend". Andreson never shows, so the two men leave. George sends Nick to Hirsch's boarding house, run by Mrs. Bell, to warn Andreson about the two men. Nick finds Andreson lying in his bed with all of his clothes on. He tells Andreson what has happened. Andreson does not react, except to tell Nick not to do anything, as there is nothing that can be done. Nick leaves, goes back to the lunch-room, and informs George about Ole Andreson's reaction. When George no longer seems concerned, Nick decides to leave town.

## Historical context

"The Killers" was written in the 1920s when organized crime was at its prime during Prohibition. Chicago was the home of Al Capone. Hemingway himself had spent time in Chicago as a young man. When things became too dangerous for the mob they would retreat to the suburb of Summit, where "The Killers" takes place. Despite Hemingway's knowledge of organized crime he omitted much of that background from the story. Hemingway himself said, "That story probably had more left out of it than anything I ever wrote. I left out all Chicago, which is hard to do in 2951 words."

## Minimalist style in "The Killers"

The basic characteristics of minimalism are:
- ordinary subject matter
- effaced authorial presence
- passive and affectless protagonist
- very little plot (in the traditional sense)
- use of historical present tense
- spare, emotionally restrained writing style

"The Killers" fit within this style in many ways. There is nothing extraordinary about the story. It is, in plain sense, simple. There is hardly any plot, virtually no character development, and very little description of the setting in the story. Hemingway also gives an objective view to the story, an "effaced authorial presence"; his minimalistic approach influenced American writing.

## Themes within "The Killers"

One theme deals with the failure of the parents of the Lost Generation to provide their children with the means to handle the cruelty and meaninglessness of 20th-century America.

Chaos is another theme in "The Killers". The many misrepresentations throughout the story create a plane of chaos for the reader, and dislocation, almost as if it is happening in another world.

Masculinity is the next theme. Although Hemingway is known for the "manly men" in his stories, in "The Killers", the two hit men are comical and clownish men. Hemingway at one point describes them as the "vaudeville twins".

## Adaptations

The short story has been the basis for several movies and a comic book short story:
- *The Killers* (1946), starring Burt Lancaster and Ava Gardner
  - This was the only film of Hemingway's work that he actually liked.
- "The Killers" (1956), a short film directed by Andrei Tarkovsky
- *The Killers* (1964), starring Lee Marvin, Ronald Reagan, and Angie Dickinson
- "The Killers" (2003), a short story manga by Mamoru Oshii and Mamoru Sugiura.

The first three films were released on a Criterion Collection DVD.

Source (edited): "http://en.wikipedia.org/wiki/The_Killers_(short_story)"

## *The Nick Adams Stories* (book)

*The Nick Adams Stories* is a volume of short stories written by Ernest Hemingway (July 21, 1899 – July 2, 1961). Hemingway's short stories which featured the character Nick Adams were compiled in one volume and republished posthumously in 1972. *The Nick Adams Stories* includes 24 stories and sketches, 8 of which were previously unpublished. Some of Hemingway's earliest work such as "Indian Camp" is represented, as well as some of his best known stories such as "Big Two-Hearted River".

### Content

The first section is called Northern Woods and includes the following stories: "Three Shots", "Indian Camp", "The Doctor and the Doctor's Wife", "Ten Indians", and "The Indians Moved Away".

The second section is On His Own which includes these stories: "The Light of the World", "The Battler", "The Killers (short story)", "The Last Good Country", and "Crossing the Mississippi".

The third section is titled War and has these stories: "Night Before Landing", " 'Nick sat against the wall ....' ", "Now I Lay Me", "A Way You'll Never Be", "In Another Country".

The fourth section is Soldier Home that has the following: "Big Two-Hearted River", "The End of Something", "The Three-Day Blow", and "Summer People".

The fifth section is Company of Two with these stories: "Wedding Day", "On Writing", "An Alpine Idyll", "Cross-Country Snow", and "Fathers and Sons".

### Publication history and reception

*The Nick Adams Stories* is one of five books published after Hemingway's death, which may have been reworked without reference to his wishes. One reviewer for *The New York Times* had this to say about one of the stories:
Alone, "Three Shots" stands as a vignette of a boy's fear, accorded sympathy by his father and impatience by his uncle. As part of the stark and spare "Indian Camp," however, it was clearly excess baggage and, knowing that it was cut out, one can only read it with admiration for the nascent and ruthlessly true artistic impulse that caused its excision. Contrary to the above are those who welcome publication of the new Nick Adams material which fills in chronological gaps of the autobiographical character's experience, and thus shows much of Hemingway's own life that remained unpublished.
Source (edited): "http://en.wikipedia.org/wiki/The_Nick_Adams_Stories_(book)"

## *The Old Man and the Sea*

*The Old Man and the Sea* is a story by Ernest Hemingway, written in Cuba in 1951 and published in 1952. It was the last major work of fiction to be produced by Hemingway and published in his lifetime. One of his most famous works, it centers upon Santiago, an aging Cuban fisherman who struggles with a giant marlin far out in the Gulf Stream.

### Plot summary

*The Old Man and the Sea* tells an epic battle between an old, experienced fisherman and a giant marlin. It opens by explaining that the fisherman, who is named Santiago, has gone 84 days without catching any fish at all. He is so unlucky that his young apprentice, Manolin, has been forbidden by his parents to sail with the old man and been ordered to fish with more successful fishermen. Still dedicated to the old man, however, the boy visits Santiago's shack each night, hauling back his fishing gear, getting him food and discussing American baseball and his favorite player Joe DiMaggio. Santiago tells Manolin that on the next day, he will venture far out into the Gulf to fish, confident that his unlucky streak is near its end.

Thus on the eighty-fifth day, Santiago sets out alone, taking his skiff far onto the Gulf. He sets his lines and, by noon of the first day, a big fish that he is sure is a marlin takes his bait. Unable to pull in the great marlin, Santiago instead finds the fish pulling his skiff. Two days and two nights pass in this manner, during which the old man bears the tension of the line with his body. Though he is wounded by the struggle and in pain, Santiago expresses a compassionate appreciation for his adversary, often referring to him as a brother. He also determines that because of the fish's great dignity, no one will be worthy of eating the marlin.

On the third day of the ordeal, the fish begins to circle the skiff, indicating his tiredness to the old man. Santiago, now completely worn out and almost in delirium, uses all the strength he has left in him to pull the fish onto its side and stab the marlin with a harpoon, ending the long battle between the old man and the tenacious fish. Santiago straps the marlin to the side of his skiff and heads home, thinking about the high price the fish will bring him at the market and how many people he will feed.

While Santiago continues his journey back to the shore, sharks are attracted to the trail of blood left by the marlin in the water. The first, a great mako shark, Santiago kills with his harpoon, losing that weapon in the process. He makes a new harpoon by strapping his knife to the end of an oar to help ward off the next line of sharks; in total, five sharks are slain and many others are driven away. But the sharks keep coming, and by nightfall the sharks have almost devoured the marlin's entire carcass, leaving a skeleton consisting mostly of its backbone, its tail and its head. Finally reaching the shore before dawn on the next day, Santiago struggles on the way to his shack, carrying the heavy mast on his shoulder. Once home, he slumps onto his bed and falls into a deep sleep.

A group of fishermen gather the next day around the boat where the fish's skeleton is still attached. One of the fishermen measures it to be 18 feet (5.5 m) from nose to tail. Tourists at the nearby café mistakenly take it for a shark. Manolin, worried during the old man's endeavor, cries upon finding him safe asleep. The boy brings him newspapers and coffee. When the old man wakes, they promise to fish together once again. Upon his return to sleep, Santiago dreams of his youth—of lions on an African beach.

## Background and publication

Hemingway in 1939.

Written in 1951, and published in 1952, *The Old Man and the Sea* is the final work published during Hemingway's lifetime. The book, dedicated to Hemingway's literary editor Maxwell Perkins, was featured in *Life Magazine* on September 1, 1952, and five million copies of the magazine were sold in two days. *The Old Man and the Sea* also became a Book-of-the Month selection, and made Hemingway a celebrity. Published in book form on 1 September 1952, the first edition print run was 50,000 copies. The novella received the Pulitzer Prize in May, 1952, and was specifically cited when he was awarded the Nobel Prize in Literature in 1954. The success of *The Old Man and the Sea* made Hemingway an international celebrity. *The Old Man and the Sea* is taught at schools around the world and continues to earn foreign royalties. Hemingway wanted to use the story of the old man, Santiago, to show the honor in struggle and to draw biblical parallels to life in his modern world. Possibly based on the character of Gregorio Fuentes, Hemingway had initially planned to use Santiago's story, which became *The Old Man and the Sea*, as part of an intimacy between mother and son and also the fact of relationships that cover most of the book relate to the Bible, which he referred to as "The Sea Book". (He also referred to the Bible as the "Sea of Knowledge" and other such things.) Some aspects of it did appear in the posthumously published *Islands in the Stream*. Positive feedback he received for *On the Blue Water* (*Esquire*, April 1936) led him to rewrite it as an independent work. The book is generally classified as a novella because it has no chapters or parts and is slightly longer than a short story.

## Literary significance and criticism

*The Old Man and the Sea* served to reinvigorate Hemingway's literary reputation and prompted a reexamination of his entire body of work. The novella was initially received with much popularity; it restored many readers' confidence in Hemingway's capability as an author. Its publisher, Scribner's, on an early dust jacket, called the novella a "new classic," and many critics favorably compared it with such works as William Faulkner's "The Bear" and Herman Melville's *Moby-Dick*.

Following such acclaim, however, a school of critics emerged that interpreted the novella as a disappointing minor work. For example, critic Philip Young provided an admiring review in 1952, just following *The Old Man and the Sea*'s publication, in which he stated that it was the book "in which Hemingway said the finest single thing he ever had to say as well as he could ever hope to say it." However, in 1966, Young claimed that the "failed novel" too often "went way out." These self-contradictory views show that critical reaction ranged from adoration of the book's mythical, pseudo-religious intonations to flippant dismissal as pure fakery. The latter is founded in the notion that Hemingway, once a devoted student of realism, failed in his depiction of Santiago as a supernatural, clairvoyant impossibility.

Joseph Waldmeir's essay entitled "*Confiteor Hominem:* Ernest Hemingway's Religion of Man" is one of the most famed favorable critical readings of the novella—and one which has defined analytical considerations since. Perhaps the most memorable claim therein is Waldmeir's answer to the question—What is the book's message? "The answer assumes a third level on which *The Old Man and the Sea* must be read—as a sort of allegorical commentary on all his previous work, by means of which it may be established that the religious overtones of *The Old Man and the Sea* are not peculiar to that book among Hemingway's works, and that Hemingway has finally taken the decisive step in elevating what might be called his philosophy of Manhood to the level of a religion."

The 2006 cover for the Charles Scribner's Sons edition of the novella

Waldmeir was one of the most prominent critics to wholly consider the function of the novella's Christian imagery.

made most evident through Santiago's blatant reference to the crucifixion following his sighting of the sharks that reads:
"'*Ay,*' he said aloud. There is no translation for this word and perhaps it is just a noise such as a man might make, involuntarily, feeling the nail go through his hands and into the wood."
Supplemented with other instances of similar symbolism, Waldmeir's criticism stands as one of the most durable, positive treatments of the novella.

On the other hand, one of the most outspoken critics of *The Old Man and the Sea* is Robert P. Weeks. His 1962 piece "Fakery in *The Old Man and the Sea*" presents his claim that the novella is a weak and unexpected divergence from the typical, realistic Hemingway (referring to the rest of Hemingway's body of work as "earlier glories"). In juxtaposing this novella against Hemingway's previous works, Weeks contends:
"The difference, however, in the effectiveness with which Hemingway employs this characteristic device in his best work and in *The Old Man and the Sea* is illuminating. The work of fiction in which Hemingway devoted the most attention to natural objects, *The Old Man and the Sea*, is pieced out with an extraordinary quantity of fakery, extraordinary because one would expect to find no inexactness, no romanticizing of natural objects in a writer who loathed W.H. Hudson, could not read Thoreau, deplored Melville's rhetoric in *Moby Dick*, and who was himself criticized by other writers, notably Faulkner, for his devotion to the facts and his unwillingness to "invent."

Some critics suggest "The Old Man and the Sea," was Hemingway's reaction towards the criticism of his most recent work, *Across the River and into the Trees*. The negative reviews for *Across the River and into the Trees* distressed him, but were likely a catalyst to his writing of *The Old Man and the Sea*.
Source (edited): "http://en.wikipedia.org/wiki/The_Old_Man_and_the_Sea"

# The Short Happy Life of Francis Macomber

"**The Short Happy Life of Francis Macomber**" is a short story by Ernest Hemingway. Set in Africa, it was published in the September 1936 issue of *Cosmopolitan* magazine concurrently with "The Snows of Kilimanjaro." The story was eventually adapted to the screen as the 1947 Zultan Korda film The Macomber Affair.

## Synopsis

Francis Macomber and his wife Margaret (usually referred to as "Margot"), are on a big-game safari in Africa, guided by professional hunter Robert Wilson. Earlier, Francis had panicked when a wounded lion charged him. Margot mocks Macomber for this act of cowardice, and it is implied that she sleeps with Wilson.

The next day the party hunt buffalo. Macomber joins Wilson in killing two of them and no longer feels afraid. The first buffalo was only wounded and has gone into the bush. Wilson and Macomber proceed to track the wounded animal, paralleling the circumstances of the previous day's lion hunt.

When they find the buffalo, it charges Macomber while he stands his ground and fires at it. His shots are too high, and Wilson fires at the beast as well, but it keeps charging. Macomber kills the buffalo at the last minute, while Margot fires a shot from the car. Her shot misses the buffalo and kills Macomber.

## Publication history

"The Short Happy Life of Francis Macomber" was published in the September 1936 issue of Cosmopolitan magazine, and later published in *The Fifth Column and the First Forty-Nine Stories* (1938).

## Major themes

The essence of *The Short Happy Life of Francis Macomber* is courage. Wilson has courage but Macomber, who is afraid of lions, has none. The cowardly husband who watched as his wife made her way from Wilson's tent hours before, reaches a point of courage when he hunts the buffalo. When Macomber finds the courage to face the charging buffalo he forges the identity he wants: the courage to face wild animals; the courage to face his wife. Tragically, Macomber's happiness is measured in hours, and indeed even in minutes. Hemingway biographer, Carlos Baker, claims that Macomber loses his fear as the buffalo charges, and the loss of fear ushers Macomber into manhood, which Margot instantly kills.

Baker believes Wilson symbolizes the man free of woman (because he refuses to allow Margot to dominate him) or of fear; the man Macomber wishes to be. Wilson understands, as he blasts the lion dead, that Margot is a woman who needs to be dominated. Jeffrey Meyers considers Margot Macomber to be the villain of the story. She characterises "a predatory (rather than a passive) female who is both betrayer and murderer"; and she emphasizes the connection between "shooting and sex."

## Reception

Ernest Hemingway poses with kudu Africa, February 1934. JFK Library

"The Short Happy Life of Francis Macomber" has been acclaimed as one of Hemingway's most successful artistic achievements. This is largely due to the ambiguous complexity of its characters and their motivations, and the debate this ambiguity has generated. In the estimation of critic Kenneth G. Johnston, "the prevailing critical view is that she deliberately—or at best, 'accidentally on purpose'—murdered him", but there are many, including Johnston himself, who hold the opposite view.

Hemingway scholar Carlos Baker calls Margot Macomber "easily the most unscrupulous of Hemingway's fictional females"; a woman "who is really and literally deadly" and who "covets her husband's money but values even more her power over him." Literary critic and early mentor to Hemingway Edmund Wilson observed bluntly, "The men in …these African stories are married to American bitches of the most soul-destroying sort." Other authors who hold similar views regarding Margot include Philip Young, Leslie A. Fiedler and Frank O'Connor (see below).

A related point that has been widely debated is whether Hemingway intended the reader to view Robert Wilson as a heroic figure, embodying Hemingway's ideal of the courageous, hyper-masculine male. Critics who argue for Margot's innocence are especially likely to question this positive view of Wilson. It is through Wilson's words that Margot's intentions are questioned, notably when he asks after the shooting "Why didn't you poison him? That's what they do in England." If Wilson is intended to be the story's voice of morality, then this implied accusation is damning. But if Wilson is a less-perfect character himself, then his judgment of Margot is suspect. Some critics have noted that Wilson chases down the buffalo in a car, violating the law and perhaps also Hemingway's code of fairness in hunting. Kenneth G. Johnston argues that Wilson "has much to gain by making Mrs. Macomber believe that the death of her husband could be construed as murder," since he could lose his license if Margot accurately described Wilson's use of the car in the buffalo hunt.

In *The Lonely Voice: A Study of the Short Story,* author and literary critic Frank O'Connor, though generally an admirer of Hemingway, gives one of the most colorful and uncharitable summations of "The Short Happy Life":
Francis runs away from a lion, which is what most sensible men would do if faced by a lion, and his wife promptly cuckolds him with the English manager of their big-game hunting expedition. As we all know, good wives admire nothing in a husband except his capacity to deal with lions, so we can sympathize with the poor woman in her trouble. But next day Macomber, faced with a buffalo, suddenly becomes a man of superb courage, and his wife, recognizing that[...] for the future she must be a virtuous wife, blows his head off. [...] To say that the psychology of this story is childish would be to waste good words. As farce it ranks with "Ten Nights in a Bar Room" or any other Victorian morality you can think of. Clearly, it is the working out of a personal problem that for the vast majority of men and women has no validity whatever.
Source (edited): "http://en.wikipedia.org/wiki/The_Short_Happy_Life_of_Francis_Macomber"

## The Snows of Kilimanjaro

*For the film, see: The Snows of Kilimanjaro (1952 film).*

**"The Snows of Kilimanjaro"** is a short story by Ernest Hemingway. It was first published in Esquire in 1936. It was republished in The Fifth Column and the First Forty-nine Stories in 1938, The Snows of Kilimanjaro and Other Stories in 1961, and is included in The Complete Short Stories of Ernest Hemingway: The Finca Vigia Edition (1987).

### Plot summary

The story centers on the memories of a writer named Harry who is on safari in Africa. He develops an infected wound from a thorn puncture, and lies awaiting his slow death. This loss of physical capability causes him to look inside himself—at his memories of the past years, and how little he has actually accomplished in his writing. He realizes that although he has seen and experienced many wonderful and astonishing things during his life, he had never made a record of the events; his status as a writer is contradicted by his reluctance to actually *write*. He also quarrels with the woman with him, blaming her for his living decadently and forgetting his failure to write of what really matters to him, namely his experiences among poor and "interesting" people, not the predictable upper class crowd he has fallen in with lately. Thus he dies, having lived through so much and yet having lived only for the moment, with no regard to the future. In a dream he sees a plane coming to get him and take him to the top of Mount Kilimanjaro as a hyena is heard from the distance.

### Film adaptations

A film adaptation of the short story, directed by Henry King, written by Casey Robinson, and starring Gregory Peck as Harry, Susan Hayward as Helen, and Ava Gardner as Cynthia Green (a character invented for the film) appeared in 1952.
Source (edited): "http://en.wikipedia.org/wiki/The_Snows_of_Kilimanjaro"

# The Snows of Kilimanjaro (book)

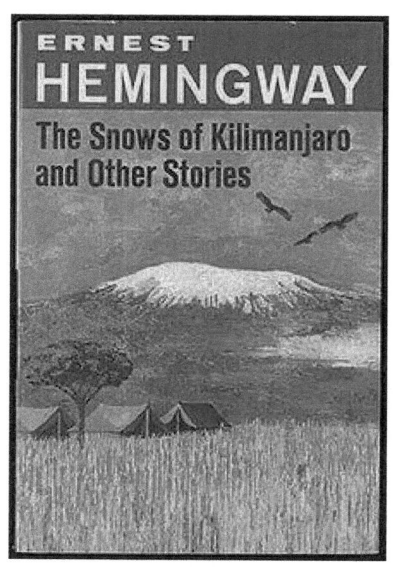

1970 reprint (publ. Scribners)

*For the film, see: The Snows of Kilimanjaro (1952 film).*

**The Snows of Kilimanjaro and Other Stories** is a collection of short stories by Ernest Hemingway, published in 1961. The title story is sometimes considered the best story Hemingway ever wrote. All of the short stories included in this book were earlier published together in The Fifth Column and the First Forty-Nine Stories.

The collection includes the following stories:
- "The Snows of Kilimanjaro"
- "A Clean, Well-Lighted Place"
- "A Day's Wait"
- "The Gambler, the Nun, and the Radio"
- "Fathers and Sons"
- "In Another Country"
- "The Killers"
- "A Way You'll Never Be"
- "Fifty Grand"
- "The Short Happy Life of Francis Macomber"

Source (edited): "http://en.wikipedia.org/wiki/The_Snows_of_Kilimanjaro_(book)"

## *The Snows of Kilimanjaro* (film)

*The Snows of Kilimanjaro* is a 1952 film based on the short story of the same name by Ernest Hemingway. The film version of the short story was directed by Henry King, and starred Gregory Peck, Ava Gardner, and Susan Hayward.

Considered by Hemingway to be one of his finest stories, "The Snows of Kilimanjaro" was first published in *Esquire* magazine in 1936 and then republished in *The Fifth Column and the First Forty-nine Stories* (1938).

The film was nominated for two Academy Awards; for Best Cinematography and Best Art Direction (Lyle Wheeler, John DeCuir, Thomas Little, Paul S. Fox).

### Cast
- Gregory Peck - Harry Street
- Ava Gardner - Cynthia Green
- Susan Hayward - Helen
- Hildegard Knef - Countess Elizabeth
- Emmett Smith - Molo
- Leo G. Carroll - Uncle Bill
- Torin Thatcher - Mr. Johnson
- Marcel Dalio - Emile
- Leonard Carey - Dr. Simmons
- Paul Thompson - Witch Doctor

### Plot summary

Gregory Peck and Susan Hayward

The story centers on the memories of a writer Harry (Gregory Peck) who is on safari in Africa. He has contracted a severely infected wound from a thorn prick, and lies outside his tent awaiting a slow death. The loss of mobility brings self-reflection. He remembers past years and how little he has accomplished in his writing. He realizes that although he has seen and experienced wonderful and astonishing things during his life, he had never made a record of the events. His status as a writer is undermined by his reluctance actually to *write*. He also quarrels with the woman with him, blaming her for his living decadently and forgetting his failure to write of what really matters to him: his experiences among poor and "interesting" people, rather than the smart Europeans with whom he has been with latterly.

Diverging from the original story, Harry does not die. Despite the unwanted attentions of a witch doctor, perhaps, or maybe his own will to live and correct his mistakes - whatever the cause, it results in his living to see morning come. He watches vultures gather in a tree as he lies in the evening. He recapitulates his life and talks to his current girl-friend. He tells her about his past experiences; then arguing, then coming to realization about his attitude, and finally reaching a sort of peace, even love, with her.

Source (edited): "http://en.wikipedia.

org/wiki/The_Snows_of_Kilimanjaro_(film)"

## The Sun Also Rises

The first edition of *The Sun Also Rises* published in 1926 by Scribner's, with dustjacket illustrated by Cleonike Damianakes. The title of *In Our Time* was misprinted in the first print-run.

**The Sun Also Rises** is a 1926 novel written by Ernest Hemingway on the experiences of the generation that came of age during World War I, later known as the Lost Generation. An early and enduring example of a modernist novel, it received mixed reviews upon publication. Hemingway biographer Jeffrey Meyers writes that it is "recognized as Hemingway's greatest work", and Hemingway scholar Linda Wagner-Martin calls it his most important novel. Critics generally agree that the novel has withstood the test of time based on style, but point to attitudes, such as the antisemitic treatment of a Jewish character, as dated.

The basis for the novel was Hemingway's 1925 trip to Spain. The story centers around a group of American and British expatriates who travel from Paris to the Festival of Fermín in Pamplona to watch the running of the bulls and the bullfights. The setting was unique and memorable, presenting the seedy café life of Paris, and the Pamplona festival, with a middle section devoted to fishing in the Pyrenees. Equally unique was Hemingway's spare writing style, combined with his restrained use of description to convey characterizations and action, which became known as the iceberg theory.

Hemingway began the novel on his birthday (21 July) in 1925, while still in Pamplona. He finished the draft manuscript barely two months later in September. After setting aside the manuscript for a short period, he worked on revisions during the winter of 1926 while visiting Schruns, Austria. The novel was published by Charles Scribner's Sons in the US in October 1926, and as *Fiesta* by Jonathan Cape in the UK in 1927. Since then it has been continously in print.

On the surface the novel is a love story between the protagonist Jake Barnes—a man whose war wound has made him impotent—and the sexually promiscuous divorcée Lady Brett Ashley. Brett's earlier affair with Robert Cohn angers Jake and he ends his friendship with Cohn; her seduction of the 19-year-old matador Pedro Romero in Pamplona causes Jake to lose his good reputation among the Spaniards. A roman à clef, the novel's characters are based on real people and the action on real events. The main theme is the notion that the lost generation, decadent and dissolute, was irretrievably damaged by the war. Additionally, Hemingway investigates the themes of love, death, renewal in nature, and the nature of masculinity.

### Background

Hemingway lived in Paris in the 1920s, where he was foreign correspondent for the *Toronto Star*, traveling frequently to places such as Smyrna where he covered the the Greco-Turkish War. During this period he gained writing experience that he wanted to translate to writing fiction. Hemingway believed fiction could be based on reality in such a way that if a writer were to distill his experiences then "what he made up was truer than what he remembered."

Ernest Hemingway (with the mustache) sitting with Lady Duff Twysden, Hadley Hemingway, Harold Loeb, Don Stewart and Pat Guthrie at a café in Pamplona, Spain, July 1925.

The Hemingways first visited the Festival of San Fermín in Pamplona in 1923 where Hemingway became fascinated by bullfighting. They returned to Pamplona in 1924—enjoying the trip immensely—with Chink Dorman-Smith, John Dos Passos, and Donald Ogden Stewart and his wife. They returned for their third time in June 1925. That year a different group of American and British expatriates went with them: Hemingway's Michigan boyhood friend Bill Smith, Stewart, Lady Duff Twysden (recently divorced), her lover Pat Guthrie, and Harold Loeb.

In Pamplona the group quickly disintegrated. Hemingway, who was attracted to Lady Duff, was intensely jealous of Loeb, who had recently been on a romantic getaway with her, and by the end of the week the two men had a public fist-fight. Against this background was the influence of the young matador from

Ronda, Cayetano Ordóñez, whose brilliance in the bullring affected the spectators. Ordóñez honored Lady Duff by presenting her, in the bullring, with the ear of a bull he killed; an honor she failed to appreciate. Outside of Pamplona, the fishing trip to the Irati River (near Burguete in Navarre) was marred by polluted water.

Hemingway intended to write a non-fiction book about bullfighting but realized the experiences of that week presented good material for a novel. A few days after the fiesta ended, on his birthday (21 July), he began writing, finishing eight weeks later. By 17 August, with 14 chapters written and the working title of *Fiesta* chosen, Hemingway returned to Paris. He finished the draft on 21 September 1925, writing a forward the following weekend and changing the title to *The Lost Generation*.

Hadley and Hemingway went to Schruns, Austria in December 1925 for the winter, where Pauline Pfeiffer joined them. During the next three months while in Schruns he worked on revisions, made a quick trip to New York to sign a contract with Scribner's, and returned to finish the second draft. He finished the final draft in Paris at the end of August in 1926, after returning from his fourth visit to Pamplona. During this period his marriage to Hadley disintegrated; alone in Paris he completed the proofs, dedicating the novel to his wife and son. By November they separated formally and Hemingway offered Hadley the royalties from *The Sun Also Rises*.

## Publication history

Hemingway and his wife Hadley and son Jack 1926 in Schruns, Austria.

Hemingway likely broke the contract with his publisher for the opportunity to have *The Sun Also Rises* published by Scribner's. He had a three book contract with Boni & Liveright with a termination clause if they rejected a book. In December 1925 he quickly wrote *The Torrents of Spring*—a satirical novella about the publishing industry—and submitted the manuscript. Unamused by the satire, Boni & Liveright immediately rejected it and terminated the contract. A month later Scribner's agreed to publish *The Torrents of Spring* and all of Hemingway's subsequent work.

Scribner's published the novel on 22 October 1926. Its first edition consisted of 5090 copies, selling at $2.00 per copy. Cleonike Damianakes illustrated the dustjacket with a Hellenistic design of a scantily robed woman, head bent, one hand holding an apple, thighs exposed. The title was decorated with apples—the intent was to have a quasi-sexual image presented tastefully. Two months later the book was in a second printing with 7000 copies sold and subsequent printings were ordered; by 1928 after the publication of Hemingway's short story collection *Men Without Women* an eighth printing was ordered for the novel. In 1927 the novel was published in the UK by Jonathan Cape.

The novel's two epigraphs were left out in the UK edition. Two decades later, in 1947, Scribner's had a boxed-set release of three of Hemingway's works, including *The Sun Also Rises*, *A Farewell to Arms*, and *For Whom the Bell Tolls*.

In 1983 *The New York Times* reported that *The Sun Also Rises* had been continuously in print since its publication in 1926, and was likely one of the most translated titles in the world. At that time Scribner's began printing cheaper mass-market paperbacks of the book, in addition to the more expensive trade paperbacks already in print. In 2006 Simon & Schuster began releasing audiobook versions of Hemingway's novels, including *The Sun Also Rises*.

In 2004 a first edition of the novel's first printing, with dust-jacket and inscription by Hemingway, was expected to sell at auction for between $80,000 and $120,000.

## Plot summary

The protagonist of *The Sun Also Rises* is Jake Barnes, an expatriate American journalist living in Paris. Jake suffered a war-wound that caused him to be impotent, though the nature of his wound is never explicitly described in the novel. He is in love with Lady Brett Ashley, a twice-divorced Englishwoman. Brett, with her bobbed hair, embodies the new sexual freedom of the 1920s, having had numerous love affairs. Book One is set in the Café society of Paris. In the opening scenes, Jake plays tennis with his college friend Robert Cohn, picks up a prostitute (Georgette), and runs into Brett and Count Mippipopolous in a nightclub. Brett and Jake leave together; in a taxi she tells she loves him, but they know they have no chance at a lasting relationship.

In Book Two Jake is joined by Bill Gorton, recently arrived from New York, and Brett's fiancé Mike Campbell who arrives from Scotland. Jake and Bill travel to Spain where they meet R Cohn north of Pamplona for a fishing trip. Cohn, however, leaves for Pamplona to wait for Brett and Mike. Cohn had an affair with Brett a year earlier and still feels possessive of her despite her engagement to Mike. Jake and Bill enjoy five days of tranquility, fishing the streams near Burguete, after which they travel to Pamplona, rejoining the group, where they begin to drink heavily. Cohn's presence is increasingly resented by the others, who taunt him with anti-Semitic remarks. During the fiesta the characters drink, eat, watch the running of the bulls, attend bullfights, and bicker with each other. Jake introduces Brett to Romero at Montoya's inn; she is smitten with the 19-year-old and seduces him. The jealous tension between the men builds; Mike, Jake, Cohn, and Romero each love Brett. Cohn, who had been a champion boxer in college, has fistfights with Jake, Mike, and Romero, whom he injures. Despite the tension, Romero continues to perform brilliantly in the bullring.

Book Three shows the characters in the aftermath of the fiesta. Sober again, they leave Pamplona. Bill returns to Paris, Mike stays in Bayonne, and Jake goes to San Sebastián in northeastern Spain. As Jake is about to return to Paris he receives a telegram from Brett, who left for Madrid with Romero, asking for help. He finds her in a cheap hotel, without money, and without Romero. She announces she has decided to marry Mike. The novel ends with Jake and Brett in a taxi speaking of the things that might have been.

## Writing style

The novel is well-known for its style which is variously described as modern, hard-boiled, or understated. As a novice writer and journalist in Paris, Hemingway turned to Ezra Pound—who had a reputation as "an unofficial minister of culture who acted as mid-wife for new literary talent"—to mark and blue-ink his short stories. From Pound Hemingway learned to write in the modernist style: using understatement, paring away sentimentalism, and presenting images and scenes without explanations of meaning, most noticeable in the book's ending with multiple future possibilities for Brett and Jake. Hemingway scholar Anders Hallengren writes that because Hemingway learned from Pound to "distrust adjectives" he created a style "in accordance with the esthetics and ethics of raising the emotional temperature towards the level of universal truth by shutting the door on sentiment, on the subjective."

F. Scott Fitzgerald told Hemingway to "let the book's action play itself out among its characters". Hemingway scholar Linda Wagner-Martin writes, that in taking Fitzgerald's advice, Hemingway produced a novel without a central narrator: "Hemingway's book was a step ahead; it was the modernist novel." When Fitzgerald advised Hemingway to trim at least 2500 words from the opening sequence, which was 30 pages long, Hemingway instead wired the publishers telling them to cut the opening 30 pages altogether. The result was a novel without a focused starting point, which was seen as a modern perspective and critically well-received.

Wagner-Martin speculates that Hemingway may have wanted to have a weak or negative hero as defined by Edith Wharton, but he had no experience creating a hero or protagonist. At that point his fiction consisted of extremely short stories, not one of which featured a hero. The hero changed during the writing of the novel: first the matador was the hero, then Cohn was the hero, then Brett, and finally Hemingway realized "maybe there is not any hero at all. Maybe a story is better without any hero." William Balassi believes that in eliminating other characters as the protagonist he brought Jake indirectly into the role as the novel's hero.

A roman à clef, Hemingway based the characters on real people and caused an uproar in the expatriate community. The early draft included the real names of the group; Hadley's character was cut early to allow room for the Brett/Jake love story. Although written in a journalistic style, Frederic Svoboda writes that the striking thing about the novel is "how quickly it moves away from a simple recounting of events". Jackson Benson believes Hemingway used autobiographical details as framing devices about life in general. For example, Benson says that Hemingway used his experiences and drew them out with "what if" scenarios: "what if I were wounded in such a way that I could not sleep at night? What if I were wounded and made crazy, what would happen if I were sent back to the front?" Hemingway believed the writer could describe one thing though an entirely different thing occurs below the surface, which he called the iceberg theory, or the theory of omission.

Balassi says Hemingway applied the iceberg theory better in *The Sun Also Rises* than in any of his other works, by editing away extraneous material or purposely leaving gaps in the story. He made editorial remarks in the manuscript which show he wanted to break from the stricture of "clear restrained writing" as Gertrude Stein had advised. In the earliest draft, the novel begins in Pamplona but Hemingway moved the opening setting to Paris because he thought the Montparnasse life was necessary as a counterpoint to the later action in Spain. He wrote of Paris extensively, intending "not to be limited by the literary theories of others, [but] to write in his own way, and possibly, to fail." He added metaphors for each character: Mike's money problems, Brett's association with the Circe myth, Cohn's association with the segregated steer. It wasn't until the revision process that he pared down the story, taking out unnecessary explanations, minimizing descriptive passages, and stripping down the dialogue, which created a "complex but tightly compressed story".

Hemingway admitted that he learned what he needed as a foundation for his writing from the style-sheet for *The Kansas City Star*, where he worked as cub reporter. Critic John Aldridge says that the minimalist style resulted from Hemingway's belief that to write authentically, each word had to be carefully chosen for its simplicity and authenticity and carry a great deal of weight. Aldridge writes that Hemingway's style "of a minimum of simple words that seemed to be squeezed onto the page against a great compulsion to be silent, creates the impression that those words—if only because there are so few of them—are sacramental." In Paris Hemingway had been experimenting with the sound of the King James Bible, reading aloud with his friend John Dos Passos. From the style of the biblical prose he learned to increment his prose; the action in the novel builds sentence-by-sentence, scene-by-scene and chapter-by-chapter.

The simplicity of his style, however, is deceptive. Harold Bloom writes that it is his effective use of parataxis which elevates Hemingway's prose. Drawing on the Bible, Walt Whitman and *Adventures of Huckleberry Finn*, Hemingway wrote in a deliberate understatement and heavily incorporated parataxis, which in some cases almost become cinematic. He skeletal sentences were crafted in response to Henry James's observation that World War I had "used up words", explains Hemingway scholar Zoe Trodd, who writes that his style is similar to a "multi-focal" photographic reality. The syntax, which lacks subordinating conjunctions, creates static sentences. The photographic "snapshot" style creates a collage of images. He omits internal punctuation (colons, semicolons, dashes, parentheses) in favor of short declarative sentences. The sentences are meant to build, as events build, to create a sense of the whole. Multiple strands exist in a story with subtexts leading to a variety of angles. He also uses cinematic techniques of cutting quickly from one scene to the next; or of splicing one scene into another. Intentional omissions allow the reader to fill the gap as though responding to instructions from the author and create three-dimensional prose. James Mellow writes that the bullfighting scenes are presented with a crispness and clarity that evoke the sense of a newsreel.

## Major themes

### Paris and the Lost Generation

Gertrude Stein in 1924 with Hemingway's son Jack. She coined the phrase "Lost Generation".

The first book of *The Sun Also Rises* is set against the backdrop of mid-1920s Paris. During the roaring twenties the favorable exchange rate drew Americans to Paris, with as many as 200,000 English speaking expatriates in the city in 1924. In 1925, the *Paris Tribune* reported that in Paris there was an American Hospital, an American Library, and an American Chamber of Commerce—it was a Paris in which one could live without speaking French. Many American writers were disenchanted with America where they found less artistic freedom than in Europe. Hemingway himself found in Paris greater artistic freedom than in the US during a period when *Ulysses*, written by his friend James Joyce, was banned and burned when it arrived in New York in 1922.

Hemingway defined the *The Sun Also Rises* themes with two epigraphs: the allusion to the Lost Generation, a phrase coined by Gertrude Stein referring to the post-war generation; and the long quotation from *Ecclesiastes* "that emphasizes the cyclical structure of the novel, the eternal order of nature, and the hope of a new generation." Hemingway told his editor Max Perkins that the book was not so much about a generation being lost, but that "the earth abideth forever". He believed the characters in *The Sun Also Rises* may have been "battered" but were not lost.

Hemingway scholar Linda Wagner-Martin writes he wanted the book to be about morality instead of writing entirely of a lost and decadent generation, which he emphasized by changing the working title from *Fiesta* to *The Sun Also Rises*. The book can be read as either a novel about bored expatriates or as a morality tale about the protagonist seeking integrity in an immoral world. In the months before Hemingway left for Pamplona, the Latin Quarter, where he lived, was depicted as decadent and depraved in the press. The novel began as a story of a matador corrupted by the influence of the Latin quarter crowd, which he then expanded into a novel about Jake Barnes at risk of becoming corrupted by the wealthy and inauthentic expatriates.

Hemingway at home in his apartment on the Left Bank, Paris, 1924

In the novel, the characters are members of a group, each greatly affected by the war, who share similar norms. Hemingway fully captured the angst of the age and thereby transcends the love story of Brett and Jake, although they too are representative of the period: Brett starved for reassurance and love and Jake sexually maimed. His wound symbolizes the disability of the age, the disillusion, and the frustrations felt by an entire generation.

Michael Reynolds says that Hemingway thought he lost touch with American values while he lived in Paris but the opposite is true. That he retained his mid-western American values is evident in the novel. He admired hard work, and showed the matadors and the prostitutes who work hard for a living in a positive manner; whereas Brett, who prostitutes herself, is emblematic of "the rotten crowd" who live on inherited money. Ironically it is Jake, the working journalist, who pays the bills again and again when the others who can pay, do not. Hemingway, through Jake's actions, shows his disapproval of people who did not pay up. Hemingway captured his time, because as Reynolds says, the novel shows the tragedy not so much of the decadence of the Montparnasse crowd, but of the self-destruction of American values during this period. As such Hemingway created an American hero who is impotent and powerless. Jake becomes the moral center in the novel; he never considers himself part of the expatriate crowd because he is a working man; to Jake a working man is genuine and authentic, whereas those who do not work for a living spend their lives posing.

**Women and love**

In Lady Brett Ashley, Hemingway created a character who reflected her time. Paris was a city where divorce was common and easy to be had in the mid-1920s. The twice-divorced Brett represented the liberated new woman. Some new women became educated and entered male dominated professions; others, like Brett, drank, smoked, and became sexually liberated. James Nagel writes that Hemingway created in Brett one of the more fascinating women in 20th century American literature. Sexually promiscuous, she is a denizen of Parisian nightlife and cafés. In Pamplona she causes chaos where she is out of her element: in her presence, the men drink too much and fight; she seduces the young bullfighter; she figuratively becomes a Circe in the festival. Critics describe her variously as complicated, elusive, enigmatic and write that Hemingway "treats her with a delicate balance of sympathy and antipathy". As a character she is vulnerable, forgiving, independent—qualities Hemingway juxtaposes against the other women in the book who are either prostitutes or overbearing nags.

Nagel believes the novel is a tragedy. In spite of their love for one another, Jake and Brett's relationship becomes destructive because the love will never be consummated. Brett destroys Jake's friendship with Cohn, and in Pamplona she ruins his hard-won reputation among the Spanish aficionados. Meyers sees Brett as a woman who wants sex without love while Jake is forced to accept love without sex. Although Brett sleeps with many men, it is Jake she loves. Dana Fore writes of Brett as willing to be with Jake, in spite of his disability, in a "non-traditional erotic relationship". Other critics such as Leslie Fiedler and Nina Baym see her as a supreme bitch; Baym writes that Brett is one of the "outstanding examples of Hemingway's 'bitch women'". Jake ends up pimping Brett to Romero, and hates himself, as shown when he says, "Send a girl off with a man .... Now go and bring her back. And sign the wire with love."

Donald Daiker suggests that Brett's behavior in Madrid—after Romero leaves and when Jake arrives at her summons—reflects her immorality. Scott Danielson believes Hemingway presented the Jake-Brett relationship in such a manner that Jake knew "that in having Brett for a friend 'he had been getting something for nothing' and that sooner or later he would have to pay the bill", while Daiker notes that Brett relies on Jake to pay for her train fare from Madrid to San Sebastián to rejoin her fiancée Mike. In a piece Hemingway cut, he has Jake thinking, "you learned a lot about a woman by not sleeping with her"; and in the end Jake likely has changed — although he loves Brett, he undergoes a transformation and in Madrid finally begins the process of distancing himself from her. Reynolds, however, believes Jake represents "everyman" and that during the course of the narrative he loses his honor, faith, and hope. Reynolds sees the novel as a morality play with Jake as the person who loses the most.

**The corrida, nature, and the fiesta**

Ernest Hemingway (in white trousers) fighting a bull in the amateur corrida at Pamplona fiesta, July 1925.

In *The Sun Also Rises*, Hemingway contrasts Paris to Spain and the frenzy of the fiesta with the tranquility of the Spanish landscape. Spain was Hemingway's favorite European country; he considered it a healthy place and the only country "that hasn't been shot to pieces". He was profoundly affected by the spectacle of bullfighting, writing, "It isn't just brutal like they always told us. It's a great tragedy—and the most beautiful thing I've ever seen and takes more guts and skill and guts again than anything possibly could. It's just like having a ringside seat at the war with nothing going to happen to you." In the novel he presented what he perceived as the purity in the culture of bullfighting—called *afición*—as an authentic way of life, which he then contrasted against the inauthenticity of the Parisian bohemians. To be accepted as an *aficionado* was rare for a non-Spaniard; Jake goes through a difficult process to gain acceptance by the "fellowship of *afición*". Hemingway scholar Allen Josephs thinks the novel centers around the *corrida* and how each character reacts to it. Brett's reaction is to seduce the matador; Cohn fails to understand and expects to be bored; Jake understands fully because only he moves between the world of the inauthentic expatriates and the authentic Spaniards; the hotel-keeper Montoya is the keeper of the faith; and Romero is the artist in the ring—he is both innocent and perfect and the one who bravely faces death. The *corrida* is presented as an idealized drama where the matador faces death, creating a moment of existentialism, or *nada* (nothingness), broken when death is vanquished and the animal killed.

Hemingway named his character Romero for Pedro Romero, shown here in Goya's etching "Pedro Romero Killing the Halted Bull" (1816).

Matadors, to Hemingway and as presented in the novel, were heroic characters dancing in a bullring—which he considered nothing less than war, but a war with precise rules in contrast to the messiness of the real war Hemingway, and by extension Jake, experienced. Critic Keneth Kinnamon notes that young Romero is the novel's only honorable character. Hemingway named Romero after Pedro Romero, an 18th-century bullfighter who killed thousands of bulls in the most difficult manner: having the bull impale itself on his sword as he stood perfectly still. Reynolds says Romero, who symbolizes the classically pure matador, is the "one idealized figure in the novel". Josephs says that when Hemingway changed Romero's name from Guerrita and imbued him with the characteristics of the historical Romero, he also changed the scene in which Romero kills a bull *recibiendo* (receiving the bull) in homage to the historical namesake.

Before the group arrives in Pamplona, Jake, Bill and Cohn take a fishing trip to the Irati River. On one level the scene serves as an interlude between the Paris and Pamplona section, but more importantly, as Harold Bloom points out, it reflects the basic theme in American literatue of escaping into the wilderness, as seen in Cooper, Hawthorne, Melville, Twain, and Thoreau. In the wilderness lies redemption and freedom. Leslie Fiedler defines the theme as "The Sacred Land", and he sees it extended in *The Sun Also Rises* to include the Pyrenees and even given a symbolic nod with the naming of the "Hotel Montana". According to Stoltzfus, in Hemingway's writing nature is a place of refuge and rebirth where the hunter or fisherman gains a moment of transcendence as the prey is killed. Nature is where men are without women: men fish, men hunt, men find redemption. In nature Jake and Bill do not need to discuss the war because their war experience paradoxically is ever-present. The nature scenes also serve as counterpoint to the fiesta scenes.

All of the characters drink heavily during the fiesta and generally throughout the novel. Writing in "Alcoholism in Hemingway's *The Sun Also Rises*", Matts Djos makes the point that the main characters exhibit alcoholic tendencies such as depression, anxiety and sexual inadequacy. He writes that Jake's self-pity is symptomatic of an alcoholic as is Brett's out-of-control behavior. Belassi writes that Jake gets drunk to avoid his feelings for Brett, notably in the Madrid scenes at the end where he has three martinis before lunch and drinks four bottles of wine at lunch. Reynolds, however, believes the drinking becomes more relevant when set against the historical context of Prohibition in the United States. The atmosphere of the fiesta lends itself to drunkenness but the degree of revelry reflects a reaction against prohibition. Bill, visiting from the US, drinks in Paris and in Spain. Jake is rarely drunk in Paris where he works, but on vacation in Pamplona he drinks constantly. Reynolds says that Prohibition split attitudes about morality, and Hemingway made clear his dislike of Prohibition. In the novel, Hemingway made a statement about his choice to live away from the US, where Prohibition was in full force, and about his friends.

**Masculinity and gender**

Critics have seen Jake as an ambiguous code hero of Hemingway manliness, yet Kathy and Arnold Davidson, in their essay "Decoding the Hemingway Hero", write that neither Jake nor the novel itself should be minimized to such an extent. There are are many ambiguities. In the bar scene in Paris, Jake is angry at the homosexual men. Elliot believes that Hemingway viewed homosexuality as an inauthentic way of life; however, he aligns Jake with gay men, because like them he cannot have sex with a woman. His anger becomes a manifestations of his self-hatred at his inability to be authentic and masculine because of his wound. He has lost his sense of masculine identity—he is less than a man. The symbol of masculine identity in the novel is Romero; but at the bullring Jake can only be a spectator. The Davidsons write that Romero reflects the core of masculinity through his bravery in facing death, and that Brett is attracted to him because of his masculinity. Ultimately Jake destroys the quintessential code hero Romero in bringing Brett to him, diminishing him and diminishing Jake's *aficion*.

Critics have examined issues of gender misidentification that is prevalent in much of Hemingway's work. He was interested in cross-gender themes, shown by depictions of effeminate men and boyish women. In his fiction, a woman's hair is often symbolically important and used to denote gender. Brett, with her short hair, is compared to a boy—yet the ambiguity lies in the fact that she is described as a "damned fine-looking woman". Her feminine traits are minimized and masculine traits are maximized. Daiker speculates that Romero may have left Brett because he disliked her image and her short hair; she lacked the womanly qualities he wanted.

Hemingway's writing has also been called homophobic. For example, in the fishing scenes, Bill confesses his fondness for Jake but then goes on to say, "I couldn't tell you that in New York. It'd mean I was a faggot." Elliot wonders if Jake's wound perhaps signifies latent homosexuality, rather than only a loss of masculinity.

Hemingway based Cohn's character on his friend Harold Loeb and immortalized him as the disliked and shunned Jew in the story. *The Sun Also Rises* has been called anti-semitic, and as Susan Beegel writes about Cohn, "Hemingway never lets the reader forget that Cohn is a Jew, not an unattractive character who happens to be a Jew but a character who is unattractive because he is a Jew." Hemingway used anti-semitic language in the novel; as a character Cohn is shunned by the other members of the group; and Cohn is characterized as different, unable or unwilling to understand and participate in the fiesta. Cohn is never really part of the group—separated by his difference or his Jewishness.

Reynolds says that Loeb should have declined Hemingway's invitation to join them in Pamplona. Before the trip he was Lady Duff's lover and Hemingway's friend; during the fiasco of the fiesta he lost Lady Duff and Hemingway's friendship, but more importantly Hemingway used him as the basis for a character chiefly remembered as a "rich Jew". Hemingway critic Josephine Knopf thinks Hemingway likely intended to depict Cohn as a *shemiel* (or fool), but that Cohn is the least authentically presented character in the book and that he lacks any of the characteristics of a traditional *shemiel*.

Hemingway's first novel was arguably his best and most important and came to be seen as an iconic piece of modernism, although Reynolds emphasizes Hemingway himself was not philosophically a modernist. In the book, he epitomized the post-war expatriate generation for future generations. He had received good reviews for his previously published volume of short stories, *In Our Time*, published initially in 1924, as *in our time*, in a small print-run from Ezra Pound's modernist series through Three Mountains Press in Paris, of which Edmund Wilson wrote, "Hemingway's prose was of the first distinction". Wilson's comments were enough to bring attention to the young writer.

Good reviews came in from many major publications. Conrad Aiken wrote in the *New York Herald Tribune*, "If there is a better dialogue to be written today I do not know where to find it"; and Bruce Barton wrote in *The Atlantic* that Hemingway "writes as if he had never read anybody's writing, as if he had fashioned the art of writing himself", and that the characters "are amazingly real and alive". Many reviewers, among them H.L. Mencken praised Hemingway's style, use of understatement, and tight writing.

Other critics, however, disliked the novel. *The Nation's* critic believed Hemingway's hard-boiled style was better suited to the short stories published in *In Our Time* than the newly published novel. Hemingway's friend, John Dos Passos, writing in the *New Masses* asked: "What's the matter with American writing these days? .... The few unsad young men of this lost generation will have to look for another way of finding themselves than the one indicated here." Privately he wrote Hemingway an apology for the review. The reviewer for the *Chicago Daily Tribune* wrote of the novel, "*The Sun Also Rises* is the kind of book that makes this reviewer at least almost plain angry." Some reviewers disliked the characters, among them the reviewer for *The Dial*, who thought the characters were shallow and vapid, and the *The Nation and Athenaeum* reported the characters were boring and the novel was not important. The reviewer for *The Cincinnati Enquirer* wrote of the book that it "begins nowhere and ends in nothing".

His family hated it. His mother, Grace Hemingway, distressed that she could not face the criticism at her local book study class where it was said her son was "prostituting a great ability .... to the lowest uses" clearly articulated her displeasure in a letter to him:

The critics seem to be full of praise for your style and ability to draw word pictures but the decent ones always regret that you should use such great gifts in perpetuating the lives and habits of so degraded a strata of humanity .... It is a doubtful honor to produce one of the filthiest books of the year .... What is the matter? Have you ceased to be interested in nobility, honor and fineness in life? .... Surely you have other words in your vocabulary than "damn" and "bitch"—Every page fills me with a sick loathing.

Nevertheless, the book sold well—young women began to emulate Brett and male students at Ivy League universities wanted to become "Hemingway heroes". Scribners encouraged the publicity and allowed Hemingway to 'become a minor American phenomenon"; a celebrity to the point that his divorce from Hadley and marriage to Pauline attracted media attention.

Reynolds believes *The Sun Also Rises* could only have been written in 1925—it perfectly captured the period between World War I and the Great Depression, and immortalized a group of characters within a narrow context. In the years since its publication the novel has been criticized for the anti-semitism, as shown in Cohn's characterization. Reynolds explains although the publishers complained to Hemingway about his description of bulls they allowed his use of Jewish epithets which showed the degree to which anti-semitism was accepted in post-World War I America. Cohn represented the Jewish establishment and contemporary readers would have understood that from his description. Hemingway clearly makes Cohn dislikeable not only as a character but as a character who was Jewish. Likewise, Hemingway was seen as misogynistic and homophobic by critics in the 1970s and 1980s, although both Bloom and Susan Beegel say that in the 1990s his work, including *The Sun Also Rises*, began to receive critical reconsideration by female scholars.

## Legacy and adaptations

Hemingway's work continued to be popular in latter half of the century and after his suicide in 1961. During the 1970s, *The Sun Also Rises* appealed to what Beegel calls the lost generation of the Vietnam era. Aldridge writes that *The Sun Also Rises* has kept its appeal because the novel is about being young. The characters live in the most beautiful city in the world, spend their days traveling, fishing, drinking, making love, and generally glorifying in their youth. He believes the expatriate writers of the 1920s appeal for this reason, but that

Hemingway was the most successful in capturing the time and the place in *The Sun Also Rises*.

Bloom says that some of the characters do not stand the test of time, writing that modern readers are uncomfortable with the antisemitic treatment of Cohn's character, the adulation given to a bullfighter, and that Brett and Mike belong firmly in the jazz age rather than in the modern era. However, he believes that the novel does stand the test of time on the strength of Hemingway's prose and style.

The novel made Hemingway famous, inspired young ladies across America to wear short hair and sweater sets like the heroine's—and to act like her too—and changed writing style in ways that could be seen by picking up any American magazine published within the next twenty years. Nagel writes about the publication of the novel that "*The Sun Also Rises* was a dramatic literary event and its effects have not diminished over the years". In many ways the novel's stripped down prose became a model for 20th-century American writing.

The novel's success guaranteed interest from Broadway and Hollywood. In 1927 two Broadway producers showed interest in bringing the story to the stage but no immediate offers were made. Hemingway considered marketing the story directly to Hollywood, telling his editor Max Perkins he would not sell it for less than $30,000—money he wanted Hadley to have. Conrad Aiken thought the book was perfect for a film adaptation solely on the strength of dialogue. However, at that time Hemingway failed to get either a stage adaptation or a film adaption. He sold the film rights to RKO in 1932, but it was not until 1956 that the novel was adapted to film of the same name with Peter Viertel writing the screenplay. The royalties went to Hadley.

Source (edited): "http://en.wikipedia.org/wiki/The_Sun_Also_Rises"

# The Torrents of Spring

*The Torrents of Spring*

**The Torrents of Spring** is a novella written by Ernest Hemingway, published in 1926. Hemingway's first long work, it was written as a parody of Sherwood Anderson. Subtitled "A Romantic Novel in Honor of the Passing of a Great Race", Hemingway used the work as a spoof of the world of writers. Hemingway wrote *The Torrents of Spring* as means to cause his publisher, Horace Liveright of Boni & Liveright, to refuse publication. Hemingway then switched publishers to Scribner's—who published his work from that time on. The work is generally dismissed by critics and seen as vastly less important than *The Sun Also Rises,* published in the same year.

## Plot outline

Set in northern Michigan in the mid-1920s *The Torrents of Spring* is about two World War I veterans, Yogi Johnson and writer Scripps O'Neill, both of whom work at a pump factory. The story begins with O'Neill returning home to find that his wife and small daughter have left him. O'Neill befriends a British waitress, Diana, at a "beanery" (diner) and asks her to marry him immediately, but soon becomes disenchanted with her. Diana tries to impress her husband by reading books from the lists of *The New York Times Book Reviews* but he soon leaves her (as she feared he would) for another waitress, Mandy, who enthralls him with literary (but possibly made up) anecdotes. Johnson, who became depressed after a Parisian prostitute leaves him for a British officer, has a period during which he anguishes over the fact that he doesn't seem to desire any woman at all, even though spring is approaching. Ultimately, he falls in love with a native American woman who enters a restaurant clothed only in mocassins, the wife of one of the two Indians he befriends near the end of the story.

## Background

Hemingway wrote the satire *The Torrents of Spring* in an effort to break his contract with his publisher Boni and Liveright. According to the contract Boni and Liveright were to publish Hemingway's next three books, one of which was to be a novel, with the proviso that if a newly submitted work were to be rejected the contract would be terminated. Written in ten days, *The Torrents of Spring* was a satirical treatment of pretentious writers. Hemingway submitted the manuscript early in December 1925, and it was rejected by the end of the month. In January Max Perkins at Scribner's agreed to publish *The Torrents of Spring* in addition to Hemingway's future work.

## Publication history

The Torrents of Spring was published Scribner's in May, 1926. The first edition had a print-run of 1250 copies.

## Themes

The hero of this novel suffers from impotence, as does Jake Barnes of *The Sun Also Rises*. Many of Hemingway's short stories from this period (such as *God Rest Ye Merry Gentlemen*) also treat themes of sexual dysfunction.

Though primarily a send-up of Anderson's poorly-esteemed but best-selling novel *Dark Laughter*, the literary proclivities of American and British close to Anderson, such as D. H. Lawrence, James Joyce, and John Dos Passos, are wound into the monkey-barrel of satire and parody.

**Reception**

Hemingway received a mixed reaction to the novella that was sharply critical of other writers. His wife Hadley believed the characterization of Anderson was "nasty"; Dos Passos considered it funny but didn't want to see it published; while Fitzgerald considered the novella a masterpiece. *The Torrents of Spring* has little scholarly criticism as it is considered a to be of less importance than Hemingway's subsequent work.

Source (edited): "http://en.wikipedia.org/wiki/The_Torrents_of_Spring"

## The Undefeated (short story)

*For the 1969 film, see The Undefeated (1969 film)*

**"The Undefeated"** is a short story by Ernest Hemingway featured in *Men Without Women*. The main character, Manuel Garcia, is a bullfighter who recently got out of the hospital and is now looking for work. After an old promoter, Retana, hires him for a fight on the following evening, he enlists the help of an old friend to be his picador. Although Zurito, his picador, strongly discourages Manuel, Manuel proceeds and is injured while fighting his first bull of the night.

Source (edited): "http://en.wikipedia.org/wiki/The_Undefeated_(short_story)"

## Three Stories and Ten Poems

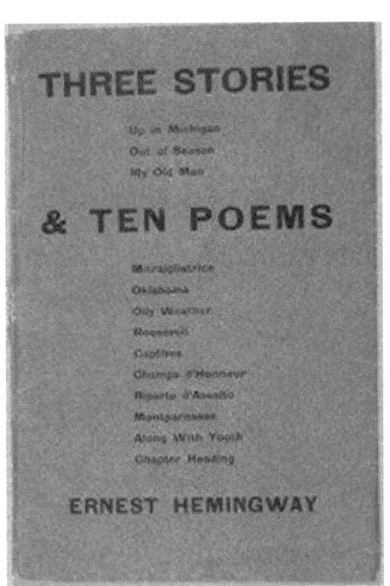

*Three Stories and Ten Poems* (1923) was the first short story collection by Ernest Hemingway; it was also his first published work. The collection was privately published in a run of 300 copies by Robert McAlmon's "Contact Publishing" in Paris, in 1923.

The three stories are:
- "Up in Michigan"
- "Out of Season"
- "My Old Man"

The ten poems are:
- "Mitraigliatrice"
- "Oklahoma"
- "Oily Weather"
- "Roosevelt"
- "Captives"
- "Champs d'Honneur"
- "Riparto d' Assalto"
- "Montparnasse"
- "Along With Youth"
- "Chapter Heading"

In "My Old Man," Hemingway used jockey Tod Sloan as a basis for the puzzled boy trying to identify the source of his father's shame, and the father who cannot divulge it.

Source (edited): "http://en.wikipedia.org/wiki/Three_Stories_and_Ten_Poems"

## To Have and Have Not

*To Have and Have Not* is a 1937 novel by Ernest Hemingway about Harry Morgan, a fishing boat captain who runs contraband between Cuba and Florida. The novel depicts Harry as an essentially good man who is forced into black-market activity by economic forces beyond his control. Initially, his fishing charter customer Mr. Johnson tricks Harry by slipping away without paying any of the money he owes him. Johnson then flees back to the mainland by airplane before Harry realizes what has happened. Harry then makes a critical decision to smuggle Chinese immigrants into Florida in order to feed his family. He kills the person in charge of getting the immigrants to Florida because the man "Obviously was far too easily persuaded to pay him more for the transport". The Great Depression features prominently in the novel, forcing depravity and hunger on the poor residents of Key West who are referred to as "Conchs."

*To Have and Have Not* is Hemingway's only novel set in the United

States. Written sporadically between 1935 and 1937, and revised as he travelled back and forth from the Spanish Civil War, *To Have and Have Not* is a novel about Key West and Cuba. The novel also addresses social commentary of the 1930s, and received mixed critical reception.

The novel consists of two earlier short stories, "*One Trip Across*" and "*The Tradesman's Return*", which make up the opening chapters and a novella, written later, which makes up two-thirds of the book). The style is distinctly modernistic with the narrative being told from multiple viewpoints at different times by different characters. It begins in first person (Harry's viewpoint), moves to third person omniscient, then back to first person (Al's viewpoint), then back to first person (Harry's again), then back to third person omniscient where it stays for the rest of the novel. As a result, names of characters are frequently supplied under the chapter headings to indicate who is narrating that section of the novel.

Legend has it that Hemingway wrote the book as part of a contractual obligation and hated it. Film director Howard Hawks, who adapted the novel for his 1944 film, claimed that Hemingway had told him it was his worst book, and a "bunch of junk". However, as Hawks' biographer Todd McCarthy points out, Hawks' many interviews contain a good deal of invention and self-aggrandizement. As McCarthy says, the director's anecdotes "go beyond ego … into an advanced realm of imagination and fantasy."

## Background

*To Have and Have Not* began as a short story—published as "One Trip Across" in *Cosmopolitan* in 1934— introducing the character Harry Morgan. A second story was written and published in *Esquire* in 1936, at which point, Hemingway decided to write a novel about Harry Morgan. Unfortunately the writing of the novel coincided with the outbreak of the Spanish Civil War.

*To Have and Have Not* is Hemingway's only novel set in the United States. Written sporadically between 1935 and 1937, and revised as he travelled back and forth from the Spanish Civil War, *To Have and Have Not* is a novel about Key West and Cuba. The novel also addresses social commentary of the 1930s, and received mixed critical reception.

## Publication history

*To Have and Have Not* was published by Scribner's on 15 October 1937 to a first edition print-run of approximately 10,000 copies. Cosmopolitan Magazine published a section of the novel as "One Trip Across" in 1934; and Esquire Magazine published a section as "The Tradesman's Return" in 1936.

## Film adaptations

*To Have or Have Not* was adapted to film in 1944, starring Humphrey Bogart and Lauren Bacall. The film *To Have and Have Not*, directed by Howard Hawks, changed the story's setting from Key West to Martinique under the Vichy regime, and made significant alterations to the plot.

The second film version, titled *The Breaking Point* (1950), was directed by Michael Curtiz and stars John Garfield. It shifted the action to southern California and made Garfield a former PT Boat captain.

The third film version, titled *The Gun Runners* (1958), was directed by Don Siegel and stars Audie Murphy in the Bogart/Garfield role and Everett Sloane in Walter Brennan's part as the alcoholic sidekick, although Sloane's interpretation was less overtly comedic than Brennan's.

Pauline Kael has claimed that the ending was used for John Huston's film *Key Largo* (1948), and that "One Trip Across" was made into *The Gun Runners* (1958).

In 1987 the Iranian director Nasser Taghvai adopted the novel into a nationalized version called *Captain Khorshid* which took the events from Cuba to shores of the Persian Gulf.

Source (edited): "http://en.wikipedia.org/wiki/To_Have_and_Have_Not"

# True at First Light

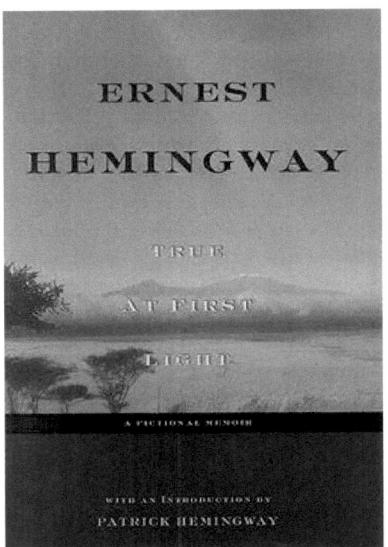

First edition cover of *True at First Light*, published 1999

***True at First Light*** is a book by American novelist Ernest Hemingway about his 1953–54 East African safari with his fourth wife Mary, released posthumously in his centennial year in 1999. The book received mostly negative or lukewarm reviews from the popular press and sparked a literary controversy regarding how, and whether, an author's work should be reworked and published after his death. Unlike critics of the popular press, Hemingway scholars generally consider *True at First Light* to be complex and a worthy addition in his canon of later fiction.

In January 1954, Hemingway and Mary were in two successive plane crashes in the African bush in a two-day period. He was reported dead by the international press, arriving in Entebbe to face questions from reporters. The severity of his injuries were not completely diagnosed until months later when he returned to Europe. Hemingway spent much of the next two years in Havana, recuperating and writing the manuscript of what he called the Africa book, which remained unfinished at the time of his suicide in July 1961. In the 1970s, Mary donated his manuscripts to the John F. Kennedy Library, including the Africa book. The manuscript was released to Hemingway's son Patrick in the mid-1990s. Patrick edited the work to half its original length to strengthen the underlying storyline and emphasize the fictional aspects. The result is a blend of memoir and fiction.

In the book, Hemingway explores conflict within a marriage, the conflict between the European and native cultures in Africa, and the fear a writer feels when his work becomes impossible. The book includes descriptions of his earlier friendships with other writers and digressive ruminations on the nature of writing.

## Background

Hemingway went on safari to Africa in 1933 with his second wife Pauline and always intended to return. Two decades later in 1953, having finished writing *The Old Man and the Sea*, he planned a trip to Africa to visit his son Patrick who lived in Tanganyika. When *Look* magazine offered to send him to Africa, paying $15,000 for expenses, $10,000 for rights to a 3500 word piece about the trip, and Earl Theisen as official photographer to go with him, he quickly accepted. Hemingway and Mary left Cuba in June, traveling first to Europe to make arrangements and leaving from Venice to Tanganyika a few months later. They arrived in August, and Hemingway was thrilled to be deputized as an honorary ranger, writing in a letter, "due to emergency [Mau Mau] rebellion been acting game ranger". Philip Percival, Hemingway's safari guide in 1933, joined the couple for the four-month expedition; they traveled from the banks of the Salengai, where Earl Theisen photographed Hemingway with a herd of elephants, to the Kimana Swamp, the Rift Valley and then on to visit Patrick in central Tanganyika. After visiting Patrick at his farm, they settled for two months on the north slopes of Mt. Kilimanjaro. During this period Percival left their camp to return to his farm, leaving Hemingway as game warden with local scouts reporting to him. Hemingway was proud to be a game warden and believed a book would come of the experience.

Hemingway at a fishing camp, February 1954. His hand and arms are burned from a recent brushfire; his hair burned from the recent plane crashes a few weeks earlier.

On January 21 Hemingway chartered a sightseeing flight of the Congo Basin as a late Christmas present to Mary; two days later, on their way to photograph Murchison Falls from the air, the plane hit an abandoned utility pole and crashed, with the passengers sustaining minor injuries. That night they camped in the bush waiting for a response to their distress call. The crash site was seen by a passing airliner that reported no survivors and the news of Hemingway's death was telegraphed around the world. The next day they were found and picked up by a bush pilot, but his de Havilland caught fire during take-off, crashed and exploded, which left Hemingway with a concussion, scalp wound, double-vision, intermittent hearing in his left ear, a crushed vertebra, ruptured liver, spleen and kidney, and burns. The explosion burned their passports, "thirty rolls of exposed film, three pairs of Ernest's bifocals, all of their money, and their $15,000 letter of credit." The group traveled to Entebbe by road where journalists from around the world had gathered to report his death. On January 26 Hemingway briefed and joked with the reporters, and spent the next few weeks in Nairobi recuperating and reading his obituaries. During his recuperation Hemingway immediately prepared the piece for *Look*. The magazine paid him an additional $20,000 for an exclusive about the plane crashes. Biographer Michael Reynolds writes that the piece, "ran for twenty magazine pages spread out over two issues", with the first issue bearing a publication date of 26 January.

In spite of his injuries, Hemingway joined Patrick and his wife on a planned fishing trip in February, but he was irascible and difficult to get along with. When a bushfire broke out, Hemingway fell into the fire while helping extinguish the flames, burning himself on his legs, front torso, lips, left hand and right forearm. Months later in Venice, Hemingway was diagnosed with two cracked discs, a kidney and liver rupture, a dislocated shoulder and a broken skull.

As soon as Hemingway returned to Finca Vigía in Cuba, he began work on a book about the safari, wanting to write while it was still vivid in his memory. He quickly wrote 10,000 words, despite his pain (eventually the manuscript grew to about 800 pages). In September 1954, Hemingway wrote in a letter, "At present I work at about 1/2 the capacity I should but everything is better all the time." A year later in October 1955, he declared: "Am passed 650 pages in the book. Am trying to write now like a good sorcer's (sic) apprentice .... always start to write as an apprentice. By the end of the book you are a master but if you commence as master in writing anyway, you end as a bloody bore." Two months later, Hemingway was bedridden with kidney disease. By January 1956, he acknowledged, in a letter written on the second anniversary of the accidents, he was having trouble remembering the trip. In 1956, Hemingway agreed to work on the filming of *The Old Man and the Sea* and abandoned work on the Africa book. He wrote to his editor, "I found it impossible to resume writing on the Africa book." Hemingway put the manuscript in a safe-deposit box in Havana, although after the 1959 Cuban revolution he feared the manuscript lost.

## Synopsis

The book is set in mid-20th century Kenya Colony during the Mau-Mau rebellion. In his introduction to *True at First Light*, Patrick Heminway describes the Kikuyu and Kamba tribes at the time of the Mau-Mau rebellion. He explains that if the Kamba had joined the rebellion, Ernest and Mary Hemingway "would have then stood a good chance of being hacked to death in their beds as they slept by the very servants they so trusted and thought they understood." The book takes place in December while the narrator Ernest and his wife Mary are in a safari camp in the Kenyan highlands on the flank of Mt. Kilimanjaro, where they find themselves temporarily at risk when a group of Mau-Mau rebels escape from jail.

The main characters in the book were based on Ernest and Mary Hemingway, pictured here at their safari camp in 1953.

The blend of travel memoir and fiction opens with the white hunter Philip Percival leaving the safari group to visit his farm, handing control of the camp to Ernest who is worried about being attacked and robbed, because there are guns, alcohol, and food in the camp. Deputized as an assistant game warden, he makes daily rounds in the game reserve, and maintains communication with the local tribes. He is accompanied by two African game scouts, Chungo and Arap Meina and, for a period, the district game warden G.C (Gin Crazed). Other camp members include Keiti, who runs the camp, the safari cook Mbebia, and two stewards, Nguili and Msembi.

For six months Mary has been tracking a large black-maned lion, determined to finish the hunt by Christmas. In subsequent chapters, Ernest worries that Mary is unable to kill the lion for various reasons: she is too short to see the prey in the tall grass; she misses her shots with other game; and he thinks she is too soft-hearted to kill the animal. During this period, Ernest becomes entranced with Debba, a woman from a local village, whom the others jokingly refer to as his second wife. From her and the villagers he wants to learn tribal practices and customs.

When Mary's lion is finally killed at the book's halfway mark, the local *shamba* (village) gathers for a *ngoma* (dance). Because she has dysentery Mary leaves for Nairobi to see a doctor; while she is gone Ernest kills a jaguar, after which the men have a protracted *ngoma*. When Mary returns from Nairobi, she asks Ernest for an airborne sightseeing tour of the Congo Basin as a Christmas present.

Ernest describes his close relationships with the local men; indulges in memories of previous relationships with writers such as George Orwell, and D. H. Lawrence; and satirizes the role of organized religion. Subjects as diverse as the smell of the pine woods in Michigan, the nature of Parisian cafés, and the quality of Simenon's writing are treated with stream of consciousness digressions.

The back of the book includes a section titled "Cast of Characters", a Swahili glossary, and the editor's acknowledgments.

## Publication history

Ernest Hemingway in Cuba with his sons Patrick and Gregory in 1946. Patrick edited his father's African manuscript in the 1990s to become *True at First Light*.

The ownership of Hemingway's manuscripts is complicated. Two books have been published from the African book manuscript: *True at First Light*, edited by Patrick Hemingway, and *Under Kilimanjaro*, edited by scholars Robert Lewis and Robert Fleming. In 1965 Mary Hemingway established the Hemingway Foundation, and in the 1970s she donated her husband's papers to the John F. Kennedy Library. A group of Hemingway scholars met in 1980 to assess the donated papers when they formed the Hemingway Society, "committed to supporting and fostering Hemingway scholarship". After Mary Hemingway's 1986 death, Hemingway's sons John and Patrick asked the Hemingway Society to take on the duties of the Hemingway Foundation; in 1997 the Hemingway Estate and the Hemingway Society/Foundation agreed to a two-part publishing plan for the African book. An abridged trade publication of *True at First Light* was to be published in 1999, to be edited by Patrick Hemingway; the Hemingway Foundation would then oversee the reworking of the entire text, to be published as *Under Kilimanjaro*. Of *Under Kilimanjaro*, the editors claim "this book deserves as complete and faithful a publication as possible without editorial distortion, speculation, or textually unsupported attempts at improvement".

In the early 1970s, portions of the manuscript had been serialized in *Sports Illustrated* and anthologized. Mary Hemingway approved the segments published by *Sports Illustrated*: segments described by Patrick Hemingway as a "straight account of a shooting safari". In a 1999 talk presented at the annual Oak Park Hemingway Society dinner, Patrick Hemingway admitted ownership of Ernest Hemingway's manuscripts had "a rather tortuous history". Access to the Africa manuscript—and to other Hemingway material—required a lawsuit and an eventual agreement with the Hemingway Society.

Scribner's requested a book of fewer than 100,000 words. Patrick Hemingway worked for two years with the 200,000-word manuscript—initially converting to an electronic format, and then editing out superfluous material. He strengthened the storyline, and eliminated long descriptive passages with disparaging remarks about family members and living persons. He explains the manuscript was a draft lacking "ordinary housekeeping chores" such as character names. The cuts made, he said, maintained the integrity of the story and "the reader is not deprived of the essential quality of the book".

*True at First Light* was published on July 7, 1999 with a print run of 200,000. For the publicity campaign, Patrick Hemingway appeared on the *Today Show* on the day of publication. The book became the main selection for the Book of the Month Club (BOMC), was serialized in the *New Yorker*, and rights were sold for translations to Danish, French, German, Icelandic, Italian, Norwegian, Polish, Spanish, and Swedish. A sound recording was released in 2007.

## Genre

In *The New York Times* James Woods described *True at First Light* as a travel journal that became a "fanciful memoir" and then a novel of sorts. Patrick Hemingway believed adamantly the manuscript was more than a journal. He emphasized the storyline because, as he explains, "the essential quality of the book is an action with a love interest". He tightened the hunting scenes, and to honor his father's statement to the reader that "where I go, you go" he emphasized the mid-20th century Africa scenes and "the real relation between people ... on that continent". Although he fictionalized the storyline, Patrick Hemingway said of the characters, "I knew every single one ... very well indeed". Hemingway scholar Robert Fleming (who reworked the manuscript as *Under Kilimanjaro*) considers Patrick Hemingway's editing essentially to be correct because he believes the work shows evidence of an author unable to "turn off the mechanism that produces fiction". The marital conflict is where Fleming believes the book took 'a metafictional turn". The published book is marketed as fiction.

Fleming considers *True at First Light* similar to Hemingway's *Green Hills of Africa* and *A Moveable Feast*—a book that presents a primary topic as a backdrop interspersed with internal dialogue. Unlike the other two books, *True at First Light* is without a preface "indicating the intentions of the author or dictating how he intended to have the book read". Fleming thinks Hemingway regarded *Green Hills of Africa* as experimental and *A Moveable Feast* as fiction. Rose Marie Burwell, author of *Hemingway: The Postwar Years and the Posthumous Novels*, believes Hemingway enjoyed writing the "strange combination of memoir and fiction". She thinks in the fictional aspects of *True at First Light* he is free to imagine a second wife and to jettison his Protestant background.

## Themes

Hemingway is "most definitely on vacation" in *True at First Light* writes Fleming; and Burwell sees an author who is willingly and happily enjoying a vacation, behaving childishly, blissfully unaware of the effect his behavior has on the members of camp. The impression is of a man seeking to delve into cultural conflicts in Africa, which takes a fictional turn in the Debba storyline. Mary is characterized as a nag whereas the character of the writer is presented as "placid, mature, and loving", immersing himself in native culture.

Burwell and Fleming says the book's subtext is about aging, as symbolized by the writer's attraction to the younger fertile woman, and Hemingway used fertility imagery to symbolize "the aging writer's anxiety about his ability to write". The images of the old elephant symbolize the aging and unproductive writer, and Burwell approves Patrick Hemingway's decision to retain those pieces of the manuscript. Hemingway scholar Hilary Justice writes the work shows an emphasis on "the writer not writing", which for Hemingway would have been a fate worse than aging. Thus, she says, *True at First Light* invokes a paradox with "an aging writer for whom writing is becoming increasingly difficult in the moment of writing about the not-writing author". Writing, for Hemingway, had always been difficult. He revised his work endlessly and stuck to the practice of writing "one true sentence" and stopping each writing session when he still had more to write. Tom Jenks, editor of an earlier posthumously published book *The Garden of Eden*, says Hemingway shows the worst of his writing in *True at First Light*: presenting himself as a "self-pitying, self-indulgent, self-aggrandizing" persona in a book that is no more than a mass of fragmentary material. Jenks thinks Hemingway is simply aimlessly writing and the plot lacks the tension notable in his earliest works such as *The Sun Also Rises*. However, he thinks Hemingway had good material to work with and some skeletal thematic structures show promise.

*True at First Light* shows the nature of mid-20th century conflict in Africa. Colonialism and imperialism pressured African tribes and wildlife. Hemingway shows an awareness of the political future and turmoil in Africa according to Patrick Heminway who, although he lived in Tanzania (formerly Tanganyika) for decades, was surprised at the degree of perception apparent in his father's mid-century writing about Africa.

Hemingway scholar Anders Hallengren notes the thematic similarities in Hemingway's posthumous fiction, particularly in the final books. The genesis of *True at First Light* was an African insurrection, also symbolically depicted in *The Garden of Eden*: "The conviction and purposefulness of the Maji-Maji in *The Garden of Eden*, corresponds to the Kenyan Mau-Mau context of the novel *True at First Light*". Writing for *The Hemingway Review*, Robert Gadjusek says the clash of cultures is "massively active" in the book with Hemingway exploring tribal practices; Christianity and Islam are juxtaposed against native religions; and the Mary/Debba triangle is symbolic of the white "Memsahib and the native girl".

Similar to his first African book, *Green Hills of Africa*, Hemingway embeds in *True at First Light* digressions and ruminations about the nature of writing, with particular attention to James Joyce and D.H. Lawrence. Patrick Hemingway explains his father was interested in D.H. Lawrence's belief that each region of the world "should have its own religion"—apparent when the male character invents his own religion. Mary's intent to decorate a tree for Christmas mystified the native camp members, and Hemingway seemed to realize that Africa was a place without an influential and established religion—a place where religion could be redefined.

## Reception

Although it was listed on *The New York Times* Best Seller list, the book received poor reviews from the popular press with better reviews from Hemingway scholars. In a pre-publication review for *The New York Times*, Ralph Blumenthal said that *True at First Light* was not as good as Hemingway's earlier autobiographical fiction, and he questioned whether Hemingway would have wanted his "reputation and last printed words entrusted solely to any editor, even a son". Blumenthal wondered about the autobiographical aspects of the work: the relationship between Hemingway and Debba; the background of the *Look* magazine photoshoot; the safari itself; and the subsequent plane accidents. In the 1999 *The New York Times* review, James Wood claimed Hemingway knew *True at First Light* was not a novel though the editors billed it as one. He believes Hemingway's later work became a parody of the earlier work. *True at First Light* represents the worst of Hemingway's work according to a review in *The Guardian*.

Hemingway with a water buffalo in Africa in 1953. The publication of *True at First Light* began to shift critics emphasis away from the image of the "white man with a gun" in his works.

Christopher Ondaatje writes in *The Independent* that the existence of a Hemingway-industry tends to overshadow his posthumous work. He considers Hemingway's African stories to be among his best although the posthumous work about Africa has been disregarded or overlooked. In her piece for *Nation*, Brenda Wineapple describes the book as "poignant but not particularly good". However, she points out that it "reminds us of Hemingway's writing at its most touching, acute and beautiful best". The review in *Publishers Weekly* is much the same saying the "old Hemingway magic flashes sporadically, like lightning, but not often enough".

Hemingway scholars think the work is more complicated and important than a cursory read suggests. With the publication of *True at First Light* critics saw a more humane and empathetic Hemingway, and began to shift their emphasis away from the image of the "white man with a gun." Robert Fleming considers *True at First Light* to be part of the Hemingway canon declaring, "This is a more complicated book than it appears to be, and Hemingway deserves far more credit for it than the reviewers of the popular press have given it. Serious critics dealing with the late works would be advised not to ignore it". Gadjusek praises the prose style, which he says is a new direction in Hemingway's writing; he also believes, despite the editing, the book is cohesive and whole with well-ordered themes. Burwell considers the edits to the manuscript generally well-done, though she laments losses that she thinks contribute to some of the subtexts in the book. Biographer Kenneth Lynn criticized Hemingway's sons for editing the manuscript but of Hemingway he says the "memorist is being totally, indeed helplessly honest," and Gray concedes the publication of the book "underscores Hemingway's courage as a writer". Despite what he considers poor workmanship in the book, Wood considers Hemingway even at his worst a compelling writer and he says the literary estate should be left alone to save the literary influence.

### Publication controversy

Many reviewers and writers were critical of the manner in which Patrick Hemingway edited the work. Paul Gray titled his review of the book "Where's Papa?", answering with the opening sentence, "He's hard to find in his fifth posthumous work", pointing directly to Patrick Hemingway's editing of the manuscript. Lynn thinks Hemingway would have been "outraged by his sons' refusal to honor his judgment that the manuscript was unworthy of publication" and was outraged that "Patrick Hemingway declares that his two brothers, Jack and Gregory, share his belief that 'this job was worth doing' ". Burwell also wonders whether Hemingway wanted the Africa book published, pointing to his statement, "I think maybe it would be better to wait until I'm dead to publish it", although she concedes that works by Chaucer, Shakespear, and Kafka were unfinished and published posthumously. During the final two decades of his life, Hemingway had published two novels but since his death, works continue to be published. Writing in *The New Yorker* in 1998, Joan Didion was extremely critical of the Hemingway family and estate for commercializing and profiting from his reputation and writing rather than protecting his legacy. "The publication of unfinished work is a denial of the idea that the role of the writer in his or her work is to make it", she wrote, adding that *True at First Light* should not have been "molded" and published.

*True at First Light* was published in Hemingway's centennial year, to a marketing campaign that attracted criticism. Hemingway's sons licensed the family name and released that year items such as Thomasville furniture with labels showing the Hemingway lifestyle—"the Pamplona Sofa and the Kilimanjaro Bed", and the Hemingway Ltd. brand which Lynn describes as "tastefully chosen fishing rods, safari clothes, and (surely the ultimate triumph of greed over taste) shotguns".
Source (edited): "http://en.wikipedia.org/wiki/True_at_First_Light"

## *Under Kilimanjaro*

***Under Kilimanjaro*** is a non-fiction novel by Ernest Hemingway (July 21, 1899 – July 2, 1961), edited and published posthumously by Robert W. Lewis and Robert E. Fleming. It is based upon journals that he wrote while he was on his last safari. It is a longer and re-edited version of True at First Light.

*True at First Light* was published in 1999. The book is a presented as a "fictional memoir". Six years later the work was republished a second time as *Under Kilimanjaro*. The work is based on a partially written manuscript, and is about Hemingway's second trip to Africa. *Under Kilimanjaro* was edited by Robert W. Lewis and Robert E. Fleming who state: "this book deserves as complete and faithful a publication as possible without editorial distortion, speculation, or textually unsupported attempts at improvement."
Source (edited): "http://en.wikipedia.org/wiki/Under_Kilimanjaro"

## Up in Michigan

"**Up in Michigan**" is a short story by American writer Ernest Hemingway, written in 1923 and revised in 1938. It is collected in *Three Stories and Ten Poems* (1923) and *The Fifth Column and the First Forty-Nine Stories* (1938).

### Synopsis

(A young woman's romantic notions of life are crushed over the course of a night).

The erotically named short story "Up In Michigan" appeared in Ernest Hemingway's first published work, Three Stories and Ten Poems. Three hundred copies were printed in Paris by Robert Almon in 1923 It reappeared in 1938 in The Fifth Column and the First Forty-Nine Stories and later still in 1997 in The Short Stories, a Scribner Classic Edition. The story is set in Hortons Bay, Michigan, close to where Hemingway spent his adolescent summers. For some unexplained reason, he took the first names of Jim and Liz Dilworth, a couple who befriended him, and gave them to the story's main characters.

"Up In Michigan" is deceptively simple, almost plotless. Jim Gilmore, a blacksmith, comes to Hortons Bay and buys the blacksmith shop. Liz Coates is a young girl who works as a waitress for the Smiths, who own the restaurant. Liz falls in love with Jim, who barely notices her. Jim, Smith, and Charley Wyman go on a deer-hunting trip. Liz longs for Jim while he is gone. When the hunters return, they have a few drinks to celebrate their trip. After supper and a few more drinks, Jim goes into the kitchen, hugs and kisses Liz, and says, "come on for a walk." They go to the end of the dock where Jim's hands explore Liz's body. She is frightened and begs him to stop, but allows him to continue. He takes her on the cold, hard dock planks and then passes out on top of her. She gets out from under him, tries to awaken him and, finally, covers him with her coat. Then she walks home, crying.she felt depressed on the way home.

As rumor has it, Hemingway may have had his first sexual encounter in a similar situation. However, it would be wrong to assume this story to be a bragging account of a seduction by a young, macho Hemingway. In actuality, it is Hemingway's first foray into the feminine psyche, a subject that will fascinate him his whole career. Liz will come to be the less sophisticated spiritual sister to the young American wife in "Cat in the Rain," to the pregnant young woman in "Hills Like White Elephants," and to the androgynous Catherine in The Garden of Eden.

Though there are two main characters, the point of view is strictly Liz's. Jim only speaks five sentences, and readers never get inside his head. Liz has fallen in love with the "things" of Jim—his mustache, his white teeth, his walk. She knows nothing about him as a person. Hemingway sympathetically explores her conflicting emotions. He understands the adolescent fantasies of this naive young girl, even as they lead to a brutal conclusion. Like many young women before and after her, she is surely disillusioned, but she will learn from her painful experience.

Jim, on the other hand, will wake up and not remember a thing.

### Characters
- Liz Coates
- Jim Gilmore
- D. J. Smith
- Charley Wyman

Source (edited): "http://en.wikipedia.org/wiki/Up_in_Michigan"

## Winner Take Nothing

***Winner Take Nothing*** is a 1933 collection of short stories by Ernest Hemingway (July 21, 1899 – July 2, 1961). Hemingway's third collection of short stories, it was published four years after his most recent novel, *A Farewell to Arms* (1929), and a year after the nonfiction book about bullfighting, *Death in the Afternoon* (1932).

### Contents
- "After the Storm"
- "A Clean, Well-Lighted Place"
- "The Light of the World"
- "God Rest You Merry, Gentlemen"
- "The Sea Change"
- "A Way You'll Never Be"
- "The Mother of a Queen"
- "One Reader Writes"
- "Homage to Switzerland"
- "A Day's Wait"
- "A Natural History of the Dead"
- "Wine of Wyoming"
- "The Gambler, the Nun, and the Radio"
- "Fathers and Sons"

### Publication history

*Winner Take Nothing* was published on 27 October 1933 by Scribner's to a first edition print-run of approximately 20,000 copies.

These stories are included in the reissued collection published by Panther Books in 1977.
- "The Short Happy Life of Francis Macomber"
- "The Capital of the World"
- "Old Man at the Bridge"

Source (edited): "http://en.wikipedia.org/wiki/Winner_Take_Nothing"